More Secondary Sc Assemblies

A resource book

Edited by Ronni Lamont

First published in Great Britain in 2009

Society for Promoting Christian Knowledge
36 Causton Street
London SW1P 4ST

British Library Cataloguing-in-Publication Data
A catalogue record for this book is available from the British Library

ISBN 978–0–281–06169–3

10 9 8 7 6 5 4 3 2 1

Typeset by PDQ Typesetting Ltd
Printed in Great Britain by Ashford Colour Press

Produced on paper from sustainable forests

Contents

Assemblies are suitable for Whole School unless a Key Stage is indicated
3 4 5 refer to Key Stage suitability

WORLD FAITHS

Contributors

Oliver Harrison has been doing school assemblies for many years. He likes the challenge (and fun!) of communicating the grace and truth of the gospel to children. Oliver's secret technique is to keep looking out for stories, metaphors and visual aids that contain and convey something about God. He uses a lot of interaction and silliness, so that the children go away laughing and, hopefully, thinking too. Finally, he always ends with a prayer, to calm the children down and to include God; the aim is to move from talking about God to talking to him.

Paul Hess is a chaplain and divinity teacher at Eton College. He writes assemblies because communicating the gospel to young people is very much part of his work. Paul is particularly interested in how that communication can be made more effective by relating it to contemporary and popular culture, which is what he tries to do in his assemblies.

Lee Jennings works with disengaged young people in a school in Liverpool. A chef-turned-youth worker, Lee is married and in his spare time enjoys eating.

Stuart Kerner is Director of Spiritual and Social Development at Bexleyheath School. He writes assemblies because he has seen so many so-called practical assemblies that don't work in practice. Stuart believes that there is a real need for assemblies with proper, interesting content, but that can be picked up and done at a moment's notice. He thinks that assembly should be one of the most educational times of the school day; it is a precious opportunity to make a whole school or year group actually think about something of vital importance.

Claire Lamont is a recent graduate. She currently lives in London and works in publishing.

Gordon Lamont is a freelance writer, radio producer and consultant. Much of his work is with the highly respected BBC Learning Division. Gordon is an agnostic who values assemblies as times of celebration and reflection on both personal growth and the big issues of life. He is the founding editor of <www.assemblies.org.uk>.

James Lamont is a philosophy student at the University of York and a freelance writer with an interest in international affairs.

Ronni Lamont, formerly a teacher of science and then dance, was in parish ministry for 16 years, most recently at St John the Evangelist in Bexley. She has co-written several titles with her husband Gordon, including *Children Aloud!* (Church House Publishing, 1997), *Work–Life Balance* (Sheldon, 2001) and *Move Yourselves* (Bible Society, 1983). Her two most recent books are *The God Who*

Leads Us On (SPCK, 2008) and *Understanding Children Understanding God* (SPCK, 2007). Ronni edits <www.assemblies.org.uk> and writes for the *Secondary Assembly File, ROOTS* worship guide and the *Church Times*. An accredited Godly Play teacher and National Society for Promoting Religious Education (section 48) inspector, Ronni also enjoys writing sermons, especially creative contemplative meditations, and working in the arena of clergy training (see <http://lamonts.org.uk/creativespirit/page9.html>).

Helen Levesley has been a teacher for four years and is Head of Religious Education at St Martin's School, Solihull, where she organizes the assembly rota. She believes that assembly provides a great opportunity to give the children a little extra knowledge that will enrich them in some way.

Brian Radcliffe is a part-time teacher and writer. He enjoys reading, writing and the outdoor life. Brian divides his time between a country cottage in the Staffordshire moorlands and a converted cowshed in France. He writes assemblies because he believes that today's students should be exposed to relevant, topical and inspirational talks. He passionately holds to the opinion that assemblies are an essential element in creating community life within a school.

Helen Redfern is a mother of five children who lives in north-east England. She loves trying to find ways to communicate universal truths in relevant, interesting and thought-provoking ways. Helen also writes on ethical issues for <www.ethicalsuperstore.com>. She enjoys books, films, TV, watching her son (and Manchester Utd) play football and writing stories.

Dan Rogers is a former teacher and Youth for Christ schools worker who is now the youth co-ordinator for a large inner-city church in Liverpool.

Janice Ross is a primary school teacher living in Orkney. She spent some time in Burundi, Central Africa, helping to establish a Christian school and now works from home, writing curriculum resources for Christian schools and home-schooling parents (see <www.schooloftheword.co.uk>). She and her husband Angus have two daughters and three granddaughters.

Introduction

I was at a conference, speaking on 'Understanding the needs of schools'. When I mentioned www.assemblies.org.uk, heads nodded, people smiling appreciatively. At another session, a teacher came up to say what a great resource the site is to her in her work as assemblies co-ordinator. And whenever I'm in schools, wearing yet another hat, there in the 'Collective Worship' planning file are print-outs from the site.

The secondary section of the site was launched in September 2004, and the number of hits soon reached 30,000. Last year we had half a million visitors to just the current, standing and rapid response assemblies. Who would have dreamed that a website could become so important to so many teachers' and ministers' lives?

Looking at the statistics, I'm reminded of the parable of the mustard seed:

> *Jesus put before them another parable: 'The kingdom of heaven is like a mustard seed that someone took and sowed in his field; it is the smallest of all the seeds, but when it has grown, it is the greatest of shrubs and becomes a tree, so that the birds of the air come and make nests in its branches.'*
>
> *Matthew 13.31–32*

I'm not saying that the assembly site is like the kingdom of heaven, no matter how relieved you were the first time you came across it! I'm more amazed at the enormous popularity of the site, and how quickly it grew, and continues to grow. Month on month, more and more people are using the site to inspire and enthuse them for the next assembly that they have to lead. The number of writers also continues to grow as assembly takers tentatively send in one of their own, to see if it's possible to share their expertise too. This amazing virtual community responds cheerfully and speedily to my 'Help – not enough assemblies for the month' emails, thinking creatively and reflectively on the issues of the day or the calendar requirements. I am enormously grateful to them for their work and commitment to the site. Thanks too to Stuart Kerner, who edited the site for its first three years, and has continued to contribute since then.

I'm also grateful to the users, who let us know their likes (and dislikes) and so maintain the two-way relationship that we now have. You are generally very positive, and communicate to us that despite loving the instant nature of a website, you still like a book to thumb through!

So here is our latest offering. All the assemblies are from 2008–9, and many of the world religion assemblies have yet to appear on the site. Enjoy! And may your leading of collective worship/assemblies flourish.

Ronni Lamont

CHRISTIAN FESTIVALS

ADVENT
What are you expecting?

By Dan Rogers

Suitable for Whole School (Church school)

Aim

To examine the meaning of the season of Advent.

Preparation and materials

- You need to prepare your tins of food. Open three different tins (e.g. beans, fruit, peas) at the top, very carefully, take out the contents and wash the tins. Now swap the contents of the tins, and carefully re-seal them using Sellotape. If you can't make this work effectively, then don't open the tin all the way round, so you have a 'hinge', and just push the lid down. It's advisable not to include all the liquid. Watch out for tin edges, they are sharp!

Assembly

1. Today's assembly is on the theme of Advent. Advent is the period of expectation leading up to Christmas. Show the three tins (whose labels say: beans, fruit, peas).

2. Ask three volunteers to open the tins. Do they find what they were expecting in the tins? What is in the tins isn't what is on the labels!

3. Ask the students: What are you expecting for Christmas this year? Invite responses.

   Give examples of unexpected presents you've received: one year I expected to get ... but I got a PC! Another year I got a ... but I was only expecting a ...

   The point is, sometimes we get things that we are not expecting.

4. Let's read Isaiah 9.6–7, which is a prophecy about the coming Chosen One of the Jews, the person they called the 'Messiah':

   For a child has been born for us,
   a son given to us;
   authority rests upon his shoulders;
   and he is named

Wonderful Counsellor, Mighty God,
Everlasting Father, Prince of Peace.
His authority shall grow continually,
and there shall be endless peace
for the throne of David and his kingdom.
He will establish and uphold it
with justice and with righteousness
from this time onwards and for evermore.

5. Based on this prophecy, the Jews were expecting their coming
    Chosen One to be a powerful military ruler, so when Jesus came,
    some were disappointed in him. Some of them even totally
    rejected the idea that he could be their Chosen One, because he
    wasn't what they had been expecting him to be.

    What they didn't realize was that what came to them in Jesus was
    better than what they had been expecting, and hoping for, in a
    powerful ruler!

 Time for reflection

This Christmas, maybe you will get what you hoped for, maybe you
won't.

Maybe your expectations will be met in the way you thought they
would, maybe they won't.

Sometimes we get things that are different from what we were
expecting.

When God is involved they are usually better than what we had been
expecting …

Perhaps you'd like to consider what you've been hoping for …

You might like to use these words as a prayer:

> *Prayer*
> Lord God,
> No matter what I want,
> no matter what I think I need,
> help me to remember that when you came
> you were not what people were expecting.
> Help me to recognize the love and care that lie behind everything
>   that I'm given this Christmas,
> and be thankful.
> **Amen**.

JOSEPH'S TALE
A nativity story

By Ronni Lamont

This story is taken from *The God Who Leads Us On* by Ronni Lamont (SPCK, 2008).

Suitable for Whole School

Aim

To hear the story of the nativity in a new way.

Preparation and materials

- You need to practise reading the story aloud. You might like to project a suitable picture.

Assembly

Settle the students, then explain that today's assembly is a story that you are inviting them to listen to.

Joseph's tale

I'd always known Mary, since she was born. Her family lived next door to myself and Rachel, and I remember Mary being born herself; the joy she brought to Jacob and Anna after all those years waiting. The faraway look in Mary's eyes as she dreamed her dreams of the past and the future, but rarely the present. Too heavenly minded to be any earthly use, was how Rachel's mother described Mary when I told her – but then she would, and I'm running ahead of myself.

Rachel was a good wife, and we had many happy years. You see the boys? Big strapping boys she bore me, and the girls were the same – tough and shrewd, a bit like their mother. Apart from Susanna, the last baby Rachel bore, for Susanna's birth was her mother's death. Susanna was small, and delicate, sensitive – not physically, but she was different. It's as if she knew that the cost of her life was that of her mother …

After I lost Rachel, Mary was often in the house, sorting for me and the children, so it seemed inevitable that I should ask for her to be my wife. She loved the children, and I knew I loved her. Shy and quiet, she would come to life when telling her stories to my brood. 'More! More!' Aaron would shout, and she'd laugh and sometimes tell another, sometimes not. For all her quiet, unassuming way, she always had the upper hand. You couldn't know Mary and not love her – there was no guile or badness about her.

Jacob was delighted when we were betrothed. Mary had been sad after Anna had died, and he was worried about caring for her – and he was showing his age. So we were duly betrothed; and then the trouble started.

I shall never forget her face, as she told me the story – an angel, she said. Special baby, she said. The Messiah.

I won't tell you what I said as I stormed out to my tools to whittle some wood and decide how to get out of this one. Except – there was a visitor in the shed. A man, who spoke of things I didn't understand, with an authority I couldn't question. The baby was special. The baby was …

The baby was due in midwinter. We had to go to Bethlehem to be taxed in midwinter.

For all her dreams, Mary could be very practical. She'd seen enough childbirth to know what was going to happen. We travelled with the swaddling bands and goodness knows what else, all in a little pack. The donkey bore her weight willingly – that donkey adored her, and the boy after he was born. But when we arrived come nightfall, and the pains were upon her, nowhere had any room, despite folk seeing what was happening. All drunk and busy. 'Go on,' they said, 'try next door.'

Thank God for the innkeeper's wife. She saw and she understood. 'Quickly,' she said, 'round the back – we've a lean-to you can bed down in. She needs to get somewhere or that baby'll come in the street.'

She wasn't far wrong. The woman assisted Mary at the birth, and within two hours he was born – big, loud and very, very beautiful. But then, all babies are.

She went back to the inn, and came back with some food for us both. The donkey settled down to sleep, and so did we, but then the shepherds arrived.

Shepherds, in Bethlehem. They'd left their flocks on the hillside, said they'd been told to come to Bethlehem to worship a new baby. And there they were. How did they know? Angels, they said.

We stayed on for a couple of months. Mary took a while to recover from the birth, and it was cold for travel so I did some repair work around the town, and we left when she felt better.

I sometimes wonder about that woman. The innkeeper's wife. I lie here now, at the end of my life, and hope that she was rewarded by the good Lord for the kindness she showed us that night.

Joshua, whom most people call Jesus now, he grew into a dreamer, like his mum. A teller of stories, but a loner. He never married – said it wasn't for him. He's a fine carpenter, mind you. I wonder what he'll do with his life. I know his brothers and sisters love him, as does Mary – for he was her only babe. Despite all our long years together, happy ones too, she never bore another babe. Without that innkeeper's wife, I wonder if he would have survived – or his mother. Small kindnesses can be large kindnesses – depends on your perspective.

Soon I shall sleep with my Fathers; and Mary and Joshua, and the others, they'll go on. On into a future that I won't be part of. I shall watch from the other side, and see what life holds for my Mary and her Jesus.

 Time for reflection

Let's think about all the babies who will be born today, and in particular for babies born to parents who are homeless.

Think too about families who will lose their babies today, through illness, starvation, or through violence.

> *Prayer*
> Lord God,
> Lover of the homeless,
> carer for the weak,
> be with all those who need your love and care today.
> **Amen.**

 Song

'The Virgin Mary had a baby boy' (*Hymns Old and New*, 496)

ST VALENTINE'S DAY
Lord Shaftesbury

By Stuart Kerner

This assembly is also found in *The Secondary Schools Assemblies Resource Book*, edited by Stuart Kerner (SPCK, 2007).

Suitable for Whole School

 Aim

To consider what love really means.

 Preparation and materials

- Prepare a large photocopy, OHP transparency or PowerPoint slide of the statue of Eros. Some good places to find a picture on the internet include:
  www.coe.uncc.edu/~sherlock/Personal/Summer2000/523517/Medium12.jpg
  www.mjausson.com/2002/img/25Jun02_London/11eros_sky.jpg
- Some Valentine's Day cards with pictures of Eros/Cupid.

 Assembly

1. Find out from the students how many of them either sent or received a Valentine's card. Tell them that although it is traditional to send anonymous cards on St Valentine's Day, nobody can say for sure who St Valentine was; and, for that matter, there is nothing to connect him to the custom of sending anonymous cards to our sweethearts – although many different theories exist. Comment that it is funny how facts and myths get confused.

2. Now ask if anyone has ever been to Piccadilly Circus in London. At the very least they will probably have 'bought' Piccadilly while playing Monopoly. Say that in the centre of Piccadilly Circus there is a statue of a winged man wearing only a loincloth, firing a bow and arrow, standing on one leg above a bronze fountain. This figure, made of aluminium, is usually known as 'Eros' (show the picture of the statue).

3. Explain that Eros was the Greek god of love. He would shoot his arrows into the hearts of gods or mortals to arouse their desires. His arrows came in two types: golden with dove feathers, which aroused love, or leaden arrows with owl feathers, which caused lack of interest. Eros would make as much mischief as he possibly could by wounding the hearts of all. The Romans borrowed Eros from the Greeks, and named him Cupid. Pictures of Eros or Cupid often appear on Valentine's cards – as the students may have seen on those they sent or received. (If you have some cards, show them now to illustrate your point.)

4. In reality, the truth is that the statue in Piccadilly is not of a pagan god at all. It is actually called the Shaftesbury Monument and represents the angel of Christian charity. It was put up at the end of the nineteenth century as a tribute to a man called Anthony Ashley Cooper, the seventh Earl of Shaftesbury. One of the streets leading from Piccadilly Circus is also named after him. Today, Shaftesbury Avenue is home to many of London's top theatres.

5. You may have heard of Lord Shaftesbury in history. As a boy, he was uncared for and mistreated. His father bullied him. At the start of his time at boarding school, his father punched his son at the door and advised the tutor to do the same. Anthony carried the mental scars of this abuse with him all his life. However, this cruelty to the sensitive boy eventually became an advantage. He was always able to sympathize with the sufferings of others.

Shaftesbury became a Member of Parliament in 1826. As a Christian, he was shocked to learn of the horrors of life for the working classes in England. He personally toured the slums, workhouses and asylums to discover for himself what was going on, before taking his evidence to his fellow MPs for action.

A list of all the social causes Shaftesbury championed would fill an entire page.

- He founded schools long before the government took responsibility for education.
- He pressed for improved sewage systems to prevent diseases like cholera.
- He campaigned to bring an end to women and children hauling coal for long hours in the darkness of the mines.
- Young boys were freed from work as chimney sweeps thanks to his determination.
- He fought against child prostitution.

- He did all he could to see that starving children were properly fed.

- He supported better housing for the poor.

All of this was guided by one simple idea. Shaftesbury was fierce in his conviction that Jesus must be at the centre of people's lives, and that through love we can all achieve our true potential. Because of this, Shaftesbury was a popular, well-loved figure. When he preached, people listened with respect. At his funeral, thousands stood without hats in the pouring rain to show their love for the man who had loved them.

6.   In the New Testament St Paul tells us what Christian love ought to be:

Love is patient and kind. It does not envy, it does not boast, it is not proud. It is not rude, it is not selfish, it is not easily angered, and it forgets mistakes. Love does not take pleasure in evil but celebrates with the truth. It always protects, always trusts, always hopes, and it never gives up.

Based on 1 Corinthians 13.4–7

 Time for reflection

Stop and think.

How do I show love towards other people?

What can I do for other people today?

> *Prayer*
> Dear God,
> Make us patient and kind,
> and help us to resist envy.
> Prevent us from boasting,
> and protect us from pride.
> Forgive us when we are rude or selfish,
> and stop us if our temper gets the better of us.
> Help us to avoid evil,
> and encourage us to be truthful.
> That we may bring true love into our own lives,
> and share it with those we meet each day.
> **Amen.**

 Song

'Love divine, all loves excelling' (*Mission Praise*, 449)

THE BENEFITS OF FASTING
Ash Wednesday and Lent

By James Lamont

Suitable for Whole School

Aim

To explore the concept of fasting.

Preparation and materials

None required.

Assembly

1. The Christian period of Lent begins on Ash Wednesday. This is a 40-day period (excluding the six Sundays) of reflection and fasting to represent the period Jesus spent in the desert, during which he was tempted by, and resisted, the devil. Christians attempt to show support and solidarity with this ideal by giving up certain things.

2. There is no set date for Ash Wednesday because the date of Easter Sunday, to which Lent is directly connected, changes every year. On the night before, tradition has it that those about to fast should use up luxury foods such as eggs, butter and sugar by making pancakes. This custom survives to this day, albeit in a more secular form.

3. If fasting is only of ceremonial value, then why do it? The immediate effects are noticeable: one saves money and eats more healthily. In fact, our society encourages this: look in bookshops for detox, diet and health-food books. Many people embark on these 'fasts' for straightforward reasons, such as to lose weight. But another effect is often experienced: an improvement in one's mental well-being.

4. Christians fasting during Lent often have a similar experience. There is joy to be gained in self-control and the rejection of short-term physical pleasures with poor long-term consequences. Lenten fasting is, for Christians, a detox for the soul: a rejection of

temptation in favour of what really matters to a Christian: fellowship with others and closeness to God.

5. Of course, giving up food is only one part of a successful fast: you should also act as you would expect a good person to act. It was the Prophet Muhammad who summarized this best, showing the importance of fasting in other religions:

    If you do not give up telling lies God will have no need of your giving up food and drink. There are many who fast all day and pray all night, but they gain nothing but hunger and sleeplessness.

6. Fasting must be done in moderation: nothing is gained from hunger alone. Muslims fast completely during daylight hours for the month of Ramadan. Meals are eaten before sunrise and after sunset. This shows that, although the fasting period is necessary, it works best when accompanied by breaks from fasting, to allow one to truly appreciate what has been given up.

7. And what about you? Do you ever fast? It does have its benefits, even if you are a person of little or no faith. So how about fasting this Lent? Give up, say, chocolate? Too hard? How about choosing something that you *can* give up successfully: perhaps give up crisps, and donate the money you would have spent on them to charity?

    Or maybe take something up, so you are giving a little of your time. Or how about deciding to be more smiley in the morning at home? Clearing up your room without being asked? Or even doing the washing-up or stacking the dishwasher? Now there's a challenge for you!

 Time for reflection

Food,
how I love it.
Give some up for 40 days?
You've got to be joking.
Time,
got so much of it,
yet I never know where it went.
Give up some time for someone else?
Give up some food to help others?
That's hard.

Do something at home?
That's hard.
Make the world a better place?

Now there's the challenge.

Prayer
Make my good deeds and actions like a ripple on a pond.
May they spread out to cover more and more people,
so that slowly and surely
the world becomes a better place.
Amen.

AN ACHIEVABLE SACRIFICE
World Vision's 24-hour famine

By Brian Radcliffe

Suitable for Whole School

Aim

During the season of Lent, students are encouraged to consider how, by denying themselves for 24 hours, they could help change the lives of children in India.

Preparation and materials

- You need a chocolate bar, a TV schedule magazine and a fashion magazine.
- Details of World Vision's 24-hour famine can be found on www.worldvision.org.uk

Assembly

1. Display the chocolate bar. Ask: What would life be like without chocolate?

   Display the TV schedule magazine. What would life be like without TV?

   Display the fashion magazine. What would life be like without new clothes?

   (*Pause*)

2. There are people up and down the country who are trying to find out what it's like to be without these everyday parts of life. At least, just for 40 days.

   We are in the Christian festival period known as Lent. It began on the day after Shrove Tuesday, which you probably know better as Pancake Day. For the 40 days of Lent, many Christians give up some luxury, ending their fast on Easter Sunday. They do this to remember the mental, spiritual and physical suffering that Jesus went through leading up to his crucifixion and resurrection at the first Easter time. Their small amount of personal deprivation is a symbolic reminder every day of what Jesus experienced.

3. Denial during Lent often brings additional benefits. If you give up some sweet or fatty treats, denying yourself can become part of a calorie-controlled diet and result in weight loss and better health. It can provide the opportunity to do other things rather than watching TV, and may improve your personal finances if you don't go clothes shopping. Most of all, stickng to your intentions for the whole 40 days can make you feel good with yourself because you've shown self-control.

4. For many children in the world, of course, it would be no novelty to deny themselves chocolate, TV or fashionable clothes. Take the so-called 'nowhere children' who live in many Indian cities, as an example. They've been given the title 'nowhere children' by the Indian government because they literally don't belong anywhere. Some are runaway children, fleeing from abusive family situations. Others are the children of immigrant families, born without an official birth certificate, so they don't exist on any register. They're found living on the streets, begging to keep themselves from starving, or they are forced into child labour with its long hours, physical suffering and pitiful pay.

5. I'd like to suggest a way that, during this Lent period, you could link a small amount of self-denial with the 'nowhere children' of India.

   The Christian charity World Vision organizes 24-hour famine events every year that children over the age of 12 can become involved in. Those taking part gather sponsors, and the money raised goes to fund a project in the developing world. In 2008 the chosen project was to set up a Street Children Prevention and Rehabilitation Programme to help at least 2,000 children in the city of Chennai. In 2009 the famine was to help children in Jaipur.

6. In some ways this is a much easier challenge than giving up something you like for the 40 days of Lent. The famine, held over a weekend, lasts only 24 hours and you're asleep for a third of that! However, in another way, it's much harder. This is a total self-denial from food: no breakfast, or snacks, or lunch, or tea or supper! Are you big enough to go for it? For most of us such a famine is perfectly achievable. There are no health risks unless you have special dietary needs. Even then you could create a special version of the famine that lasts for a few hours.

Time for reflection

World Vision's 24-hour famine may not be your cup of tea (you *are* allowed drinks during the famine). The principle at the heart of Lent is a good one, however, especially if your own self-denial can lead to the benefit of someone more needy than you are. Why not create a simple Lent response for yourself? You could:

- Give the price of a chocolate bar to a charity you sympathize with.
- Miss your favourite soap opera for a week and visit a relative, or lonely person instead.
- Sort through your clothes and take those you no longer wear to a charity shop.
- Buy a copy of *The Big Issue* instead of your usual magazine.
- Or maybe you've got a better idea?!

Spend a moment considering the following thoughts. You may wish to turn them into a prayer:

Be thankful for whatever gives you most pleasure (it may be food, people, places, music, a piece of technology or something else).

Be sorry for those times this week when you've thought more about what you wanted than the needs of others.

Make a plan to take some action that arises out of today's assembly.

 Suggested music

Play the track 'Something Inside So Strong' by Labi Siffre.

EASTER
A *Star Wars* reflection

By Ronni Lamont

Suitable for Whole School

Aim

To explore the concept of death and resurrection through parallels between the film *Star Wars* and the Easter story.

Preparation and materials

- You need a recording of the theme to *Star Wars*; available from download sites, or on CD.

Assembly

1. Play the *Star Wars* theme music as the students gather.

    Easter can be a difficult festival to get your head around. The story of a man being killed and then coming back to life is not only unique; for us, it is sometimes impossible to believe. I'd like to suggest that the original *Star Wars* film contains material that is helpful to us as we struggle to comprehend the claims of the Easter story.

2. If you've never seen the original film, confusingly called Episode IV, and released in 1977, then here's a précis:

    'A long time ago in a galaxy far far away ...' Our hero is a young man called Luke Skywalker. He lives with his aunt and uncle but dreams of being a fighter pilot, fighting with the rebels against the evil Empire. His uncle buys two robot 'droids', one of which runs away, and in the search for the droid, R2-D2, Luke meets the mysterious hermit, Ben Kenobi, whom we later discover is actually a Jedi knight, Obi-Wan Kenobi.

    When they get back to the farm, they find that Luke's aunt and uncle have been murdered by imperial storm troopers, who were searching for the droids.

    Luke discovers a film message hidden within the droid, and he heads off, with Ben, to find the sender of the message, Princess

Leia, who is being held captive by the Empire on a huge satellite, the Death Star.

Luke, aided and abetted by Han Solo, the captain of the ship they've been travelling on, rescues the princess, but as they are running back to the spaceship to escape, Ben goes into battle with the arch-baddie, Darth Vader, a fallen Jedi knight who now serves the evil Empire. The two Jedi knights, Ben and Darth Vader, fight a duel, using light sabres, a sort of laser sword.

Luke turns around to wait for Ben, who looks at Luke calmly, then says to Darth Vader: 'If you strike me down, I shall become more powerful than you can possibly imagine.' He stands, looks at Darth Vader, and is cut down by Vader's light sabre. However, as he falls down dead, it is evident that there is no body, just a heap of clothes, and we hear his voice urging: 'Run, Luke, run.' Luke runs, they take off, and the story gallops away again.

3. Towards the end of the film, Luke is flying in the attack to destroy the Death Star. The lives of a whole planet, Princess Leia's home, will be lost if the mission fails. As he flies into the heart of the satellite, he hears Ben's voice once more, urging him to 'feel the Force'. He turns off his radar, concentrates … and I don't want to spoil the ending, but you can probably guess!

At the very end of the story, we see a ghostly Ben, smiling at Luke and the others.

4. The whole story pivots around Ben's death. Ben dies, and so the spaceship containing Luke, Han Solo and the princess can escape and they return to destroy the Death Star. There is the straight parallel of an innocent man dying to set the others, quite literally, free.

But notice what Ben said as Darth Vader killed him: 'If you strike me down I shall become more powerful than you can possibly imagine.'

5. Through the next two films, Episodes V and VI, Ben keeps cropping up – you never know where he will be next, as he's not confined to any one physical place. No matter where Luke goes, so Ben continues to guide and help him. By letting go of his physical body, Ben's essence, perhaps his spirit, is liberated to be wherever Luke needs him.

6. So it is at Easter. Jesus dies, but then, later on, his friends, his disciples, claim to have seen him again. He can walk through

walls, be in two places almost at the same time – clearly recognizable, but not contained within his previous physical body. It is just the same as we see in the film for Ben. Death is not the end, but in some way the beginning of a new, unconstrained life, where the person who died is now free to be wherever they are needed – throughout the whole of space in the case of Ben, or for Jesus, across the planet.

7. So, this Easter, when you struggle to think about the claims of Christians about the death and new life of Jesus, perhaps you can think of Obi-Wan, Ben Kenobi, and remember: 'If you strike me down I shall become more powerful than you can possibly imagine.' For he certainly was.

 Time for reflection

Prayer
Now the green blade riseth
From the buried grain
Wheat, that in the dark earth
Many days hath lain.
Love lives again
Like wheat that sleeps unseen
Love is come again
Like wheat, that springeth green.
Amen.
John Crum, 1928

GOING UP!
Ascension Day

By Stuart Kerner

Suitable for Key Stage 3

 Aim

To consider the meaning behind the Christian festival of Ascension.

 Preparation and materials

- If you have access to a digital projector and the internet you might like to show the launch of Apollo 11. It is available quite readily on sites like YouTube, TeacherTube and the Smithsonian National Air and Space Museum.
- Bible references: Matthew 28.16–20; Mark 16.19–20; Luke 24.44–53; Acts 1.6–11.

 Assembly

1. Have you ever watched footage of a space shuttle or a rocket taking off? The countdown ... the eager anticipation ... the slight fear that something might go wrong, or else that it might not even take off.

   If and when the spacecraft does manage to become airborne we are treated to an amazing spectacle of both power and grace ... the commanding roar of the engines ... the phenomenal sight of all that rocket fuel being ignited ... and eventually the majestic vehicle ascending, up and away ... hurtling into space ... until it can no longer be seen by the naked eye.

2. Unfortunately, in the twenty-first century we have become a little blasé about space travel, and watching rockets take off is no longer the massive draw it once was, say, in the late 1960s, as humankind reached ever nearer the moon. That was 40 years ago and sadly familiarity has largely bred contempt in an age when rich people can now simply buy their way to the stars.

3. In some ways this indifference to things ascending is a little like some people's attitudes towards the Christian festival known as Ascension. Although it is one of the four most important Christian

dates, along with Christmas, Easter and Pentecost, it remains something of a 'poor relation'.

4. Ascension is described in three of the Gospels and the book of Acts. It is the time when Christians remember how Jesus, who had beaten death and risen at Easter, led his followers to the top of a hill overlooking Jerusalem and promised that he would always be with them and that the Holy Spirit would also come to look after them; before instructing them to go out to the whole world and spread the good news about everything he had done.

    When he had done this, a cloud came down and settled over the hilltop and Jesus vanished! Typically it's described as Jesus being taken up into heaven. His earthly work was complete.

5. In many ways Ascension is a rather neglected point in the Church calendar, squeezed between Easter and Pentecost, the festival which follows ten days later.

    For a start, it is properly celebrated on the Thursday that falls 40 days after Easter, to reflect the fact that the resurrected Jesus remained with his disciples for 40 days after he rose from the dead. In recent years, however, it has become the practice in some churches to mark it on the Sunday after this Thursday to make it more convenient for worshippers.

    In some churches the Paschal candle that has burned since Easter is put out and in others a statue of Jesus is hoisted through a hole in the church roof!

6. The real problem with Ascension is that it heralds a time of waiting. After the excitement of Easter, with all its high points and low points, miracles and wonders, Ascension is Jesus laying the foundations for his Church and promising great things to come.

    Jesus' promise of a glorious future when he returns is as tantalizing as any promise ever made. Unfortunately most people hate waiting for good things.

7. The Ascension is crucial to the hope Christians place in Jesus: they say that he died for our sins and was raised to life, but without the Ascension we cannot claim with confidence that God has raised us up with Christ Jesus and seated us with him in heaven.

    And there is then a permanent link between the ascension and the coming of God's kingdom: the two men in white robes who appeared to the disciples at the ascension told them that Jesus would come again in the same way that they saw him go.

8.   It is God's way of saying, 'I've started, so I'll finish.' The coming of Jesus set something in motion that is unstoppable, and we are caught up in eternity, we share the heavenly feast and can taste the future that God has promised us.

That is only possible because Christ has ascended and taken his, and thus our, humanity into heaven. Perhaps we should reconsider our attitude towards space flight after all!

 Time for reflection

As a telescope focuses our eyes on the vastness of space,
so we look forward to the return of Christ.
As a rocket touches the sky,
so we touch heaven through the Ascension of Christ.
As astronauts seek out discovery beyond the stars,
so we find salvation through the Ascension of Christ.

> *Prayer*
> Blessed are you,
> God of heaven and earth,
> to you be glory and honour for ever.
> From the darkness of death
> you have raised your Son
> to sit at your right hand in majesty.
> The founder of our faith,
> his passion accomplished,
> has shown us the way to heaven
> and gives us the promised Spirit.
> May we be ready to follow your Way
> and so be brought to the glory of his presence
> where songs of victory for ever sound:
> Blessed be God, Father, Son and Holy Spirit.
> **Amen.**

Evening Prayer for Ascension, adapted from Common Worship

 Song

'When from the sky' (*Come and Praise*, 132)

EXPECT THE UNEXPECTED!
Pentecost

By Lee Jennings

Suitable for Key Stage 3

Aim

God promises to be always with us. Expect the unexpected!

Preparation and materials

- Prepare some presents containing items that people may not expect (e.g. a big, exciting looking present with a disappointing gift inside).
- One present should be a small scruffy box, with some money inside it.

Assembly

1. Invite a few volunteers up to the front and ask them to each choose a present. Ask them why they chose that particular one.

2. One at a time, allow them to open their present, asking how they felt when they saw the gift inside. Most should feel disappointed. Or annoyed at you for stitching them up! Finally, let the volunteer with the small scruffy box open theirs. Ask them how they felt at getting a good prize.

   Thank the volunteers for their help.

3. One day Jesus was going to Jerusalem, and he rode into the city on a donkey. People were excited that he was coming; they went out on to the streets to see him and they waved palm branches.

   The only problem was, the Jews were expecting a king who would come to set them free from the Romans. They didn't think Jesus really looked like the person who was going to save them. Because of this, they thought he wasn't telling the truth, and some of them took Jesus to court. They tried him, and then decided to kill him. They expected something, but were disappointed with what they got.

4. However, Jesus came back to life again, which was an even bigger surprise to his friends. Instead of being disappointed, we can be really happy that Jesus loves us and cares for us. God brought Jesus back from the dead, something we remembered at Easter. Christians believe that Jesus is still alive, and cares for each one of us.

5. Sometimes in life, we don't always get what we expect. Sometimes people let us down, and sometimes we can feel that God has let us down. But God promises that he will never leave us. When Jesus came alive again, he said that he would send his Holy Spirit to be with us and to help us, so that he could always be with us. This is what Christians remember at Pentecost: Jesus sending his Holy Spirit to be a helper for Christians in every aspect of their lives.

 Time for reflection

Mother Julian, a woman who lived in Norwich many centuries ago, said that God gave her a vision. In her vision she was holding something about the size of a hazelnut. When she asked God what it was, God replied that it was everything that was made. When she asked God about the sadness that people live with, God replied: 'All shall be well and all shall be well and all manner of thing shall be well.'

Prayer
Lord God,
Thank you that you promised to be with us always.
Thank you that you promise that all will be well.
Help me to remember that, no matter what.
Amen.

PENTECOST POWER
'You could be my witnesses!'

By Janice Ross

Suitable for Key Stage 3

Aim

The story of Pentecost shows that we need the power of God's Holy Spirit to enable us to live as Jesus did and to be his disciples.

Preparation and materials

- This assembly contains lots of resources: you may want to omit one or two of the sections contained within it.
- You will need three teachers to read the script: Interviewer, Andrew Lloyd Webber, Jesus.
- Six pupils to read the Bible verses.

Assembly

1. Most of the students will be familiar with *I'd Do Anything*, the 2008 TV programmes featuring Andrew Lloyd Webber and his search for three 'Olivers' and a 'Nancy' to star in the West End production of *Oliver!*. *Oliver!* is based on Charles Dickens' book *Oliver Twist*, which tells the story of a young orphan boy who gets involved with a gang of pickpockets in nineteenth-century London.

   But for those who didn't see the programmes here is a summary. Some years ago Andrew Lloyd Webber took on the challenge of putting on the musical *The Sound of Music*. Young women were invited to audition for the part of Maria, which had been played in the film by Julie Andrews. Numbers were whittled down and eventually 12 hopefuls were accepted into 'the house' to be prepared for the part. Week by week one was voted off until a new Maria was discovered, in the form of Connie Fisher.

   The following year we saw a new star who was given the part of Joseph for the musical *Joseph and the Amazing Technicolor Dreamcoat*. His name was Lee Mead.

And this time Andrew Lloyd Webber wanted three Olivers (the number of performances would be too gruelling for one boy) and one Nancy.

2. In initial auditions hundreds of hopefuls tried for the part of Nancy. Ask the students what kind of character the judges were looking for? (A quote from Andrew Lloyd Webber: 'A girl of the street and yet she has a heart of gold underneath it all. We're looking for a girl who really is a rough diamond.')

    One by one the young women were asked to leave because they were 'too young, too middle class, too sweet' or they just couldn't sing! Those who made it were told, 'You could be a Nancy.'

    In the Nancy House, 12 hopefuls were taught to sing, act, talk, walk, think like a Nancy. At the end of ten weeks of training, voting and 'sing-offs', the eventual winner was Jodie Prenger.

3. Now ask the children to picture a different house. This one is an upper room in first-century Jerusalem. Twelve men had been chosen, but they had been reduced to 11. (One had killed himself, because he was responsible for the death of an innocent man, Jesus.)

    Their task is going to be to take the message of Christianity to the whole world. They have followed Jesus of Nazareth for three years. Now they have 50 days to become the part, 50 days to become like Jesus, to be called Christians!

4. Ask the students to listen to the following interview and to think about whether they would take on any of these men if they were auditioning for the part of a Christian (which simply means a witness to, or disciple of, Jesus)?

    On the third day after his death the miraculous had happened, just as Jesus had said it would, although the disciples had not understood this teaching at the time. Jesus had risen from the dead. The disciples were now sitting with him, huddled in an upstairs room out of sight of the religious and Roman authorities. They were still very afraid that they might be next in line for crucifixion.

    They talked with him, ate with him and marvelled as he went over the ancient scriptures once again and opened their eyes to the truth of God's word.

Then he said to them, 'You will be my witnesses.' Not: 'You could be my witnesses' but: 'You will be my witnesses'!

Interviewer: So, who have you got lined up in the Nancy House, Andrew?

ALW: I'd say a very promising group. Some have real musical talent. There's one I have my eye on who already talks and acts like a Nancy and then there is another who for her age has a remarkable ability to put herself in Nancy's shoes.

Interviewer: And what about you, Jesus? What about your group?

Jesus: Well, I suppose you would call them uneducated, rough men on the whole. Some are fishermen. Some, like the converted tax collector, Matthew, have not been very popular. They are nothing much to look at. Peter can be a bit of a hothead and James and John are rightly nicknamed Sons of Thunder.

Interviewer: Mmm. Interesting! What about experience, Andrew? Have many of your girls been on the stage before?

ALW: Yes, they have. One has been in opera, many in beauty pageants, and local singing talent shows. I am finding that more and more of our contestants have some sort of training in the performing arts.

Interviewer: So you have something to work on. What about your 11, Jesus?

Jesus: They have certainly spent three years watching me at work and listening to my teaching. They have had a bit of practice themselves too. I sent them out two by two and they found themselves doing some of the things I could do. They travelled about with only the clothes they stood up in and yet they were provided for. They prayed for the sick and saw them healed.

Interviewer: That's excellent! And Andrew, there is no doubt that your girls were desperate for the job! Everyone watching the programme saw the tears and heard the screams of delight when you uttered those famous words, 'You could be a Nancy!' I suppose, Jesus, the same could be said for your disciples?

Jesus: Well no, not exactly.

Interviewer: What do you mean?

Jesus: Well, they had been convinced for a while that I was the

Messiah, promised from of old, and they gave up everything to follow me. But it all came to an end. I angered the religious leaders and our own people were responsible for my death, as you know. In the end my friends fled. The strongest of them even denied knowing me. They are no longer convinced that they want to be disciples. They are gripped by fear, and they have been hiding behind locked doors. Can you blame them?

Interviewer: I see. No, I am not sure I do blame them. But now you are back, things will be fine again.

Jesus: But I am not staying. And life will not be easy for my friends.

Interviewer: Oh, so they are going to have to train very hard in the house over the next few weeks. You are going to have to knock some discipline into them. I don't envy you your task.

Jesus: No, my friend, it won't exactly be like that. That's not the way it will work at all!

5.   Did it work for these disciples? Were they successfully turned into witnesses of Jesus?

Ask six students to read the following words from Acts, the book in the Bible that tells the story of the early Church.

Reader 1: Do not leave Jerusalem, but wait for the gift my Father promised, which you have heard me speak about. You will receive power when the Holy Spirit comes on you, and you will be my witnesses in Jerusalem and in all Judea and Samaria, and to the ends of the earth.

Reader 2: When the day of Pentecost came … all of them were filled with the Holy Spirit.

Reader 3: Those who accepted Peter's message were baptized, and about three thousand were added to their number that day.

Reader 4: When the rulers, elders and teachers of the law saw the courage of Peter and John and realized that they were unschooled, ordinary men, they were astonished.

Reader 5: Persecution broke out against the church at Jerusalem and they were scattered. Those who had been scattered preached the word wherever they went.

Reader 6: In Thessalonica Paul and Silas were dragged before the city officials. 'These men who are turning the world upside down have now come here!'

Time for reflection

Often we try to be like Jesus using our own strength and by our own efforts, and fail miserably! What difference does the Pentecost story mean for us today?

Prayer

Dear God,

Thank you that you know our weakness and lack of strength often to do what is right.

Thank you that you indeed helped these eleven men to be your witnesses to the ends of the earth.

Thank you that today you are still helping thousands of ordinary often uneducated men and women, girls and boys to be your disciples.

Amen.

THUNDERBIRDS ARE GO!
Trinity Sunday

By Ronni Lamont

Suitable for Keyf Stage 3

Aim

To use the TV programme *Thunderbirds* as a model for the Trinity.

Preparation and materials

- *Thunderbirds* toys would be good visual aids. They are still available (try www.amazon.co.uk), but if you ask around, you may find that younger siblings still have these toys at home.

Assembly

1. Trinity Sunday occurs eight weeks after Easter Sunday. It is the day when the Christian Church reflects on the nature of God. The Church refers to God as 'Trinity', i.e. three persons who are one God. We call them the Father, the Son and the Holy Spirit. This is heavy-duty thinking, so here's a way to think about the Trinity that you may find helpful.

2. Many years ago, you may have watched a TV series called *Thunderbirds*. It was originally shown in the 1960s but has been repeated many, many times. The toys from the show are still available, and so are DVDs of the series. Not so long ago a feature film was made, and there's also been a stage show.

   If you never saw the series, you may like to know that it's made with puppets – marionettes, the type with strings. It's about the Tracy family who live on a remote island in the Pacific: the father, Jeff, who has five sons – Scott, Virgil, Gordon, John and Alan – and Jeff's mother, Grandma, whose only role seems to be making coconut crumble! Also living on the island are a servant, Kyrano, and his daughter Tin-Tin; and Brains, a genius designer and builder of planes, spaceships and rescue vehicles of every shape and size. The other person we meet is the very English Lady Penelope and her ex-convict butler, Parker.

Jeff runs the family business, which is top secret, called International Rescue. This organization picks up distress calls from around the world via its own satellite. These are radioed to HQ, and then the Thunderbirds are launched!

Scott goes first on Thunderbird 1. He flies in and sets up a mobile HQ, so that when Virgil arrives in the heavy transporter plane, Thunderbird 2, the rescue can begin.

The rescue always has moments of drama and high tension, especially if Kyrano's evil half-brother, 'The Hood', contacts him through a weird psychic trance to try and sabotage the rescue attempt. Lady Penelope usually joins in the action, giving chase in her pink Rolls-Royce. Finally, all is well; at the end the people are saved, and International Rescue vanishes back to paradise – until the next call for help.

3. So what's this got to do with God? Well, let's look at how International Rescue works: Jeff, the father, stays at HQ. The sons go out to rescue people. They communicate by radio. You might like to think of God as the Father, in heaven. God sees that people need help, so he sends his Son, Jesus, who lives with people and shows us how to be like God. His relationship to God the Father becomes clear through his death and resurrection – which we thought about over Easter. Christians believe that Jesus saves people from the wrong things that they have done, bringing them back to a good relationship with God.

    And the Holy Spirit is like the radio – the carrier of the message from the Father (Jeff or God) to the Son (Jesus or Scott, Virgil and co.). Christians believe that it's the Holy Spirit living within them who helps them to be close to God day by day. Without the radio, International Rescue couldn't communicate. Without the Holy Spirit, Christians can't pray – their way of communicating with God.

 Time for reflection

Think about International Rescue, flying out to save people from the disasters that they've been caught up in.

Reflect on the claims of Jesus, sent by God the Father to bring us back to God.

Prayer
God:
Father
Son
and Holy Spirit.
I don't understand how that works,
but I believe that you are there for me,
saving me and helping me
day by day.

Be close to each of us today.
Help us to work at our relationships with each other
and with you.
Amen.

 Song

'Spirit of God' (*Come and Praise*, 63)

'CRY GOD FOR HARRY, ENGLAND AND ST GEORGE!'
St George's Day (23 April)

By Ronni Lamont

Suitable for Whole School

Aim

To think about those who suffer for their faith, and standing up for what you believe in.

Preparation and materials

- A flag of St George would be useful, even if it's just a small one, the type that are available during international football/rugby tournaments.
- As the students arrive, play some patriotic English music, perhaps 'Jerusalem' by Parry, or 'Land of Hope and Glory'. 'Nimrod' from the *Enigma Variations* by Elgar is used in the reflection.

Assembly

1. You will all be familiar with this flag (wave flag). During big sporting events, people fix them to their cars as they drive around. The flags are sometimes displayed from houses. Then, when England lose, we despondently put them away until next time.

   This is the flag of St George, the patron saint of England. The trouble is, he wasn't English, and because he died many years ago, his story has been embroidered and the truth lost in history. But there is one bit that most people agree is true.

2. St George was a high-ranking soldier in the Roman army, who died during the reign of the Emperor Diocletian, in about AD 303. He was a Christian, and the Emperor was persecuting Christians at that time. George was horribly tortured, but would not deny his faith; eventually he was beheaded near the town of Lydda in Palestine, present-day Israel. Later on his head was taken to Rome and buried in a church that was then dedicated to George.

3. Stories about his bravery soon spread. The crusading knights of the Middle Ages heard the stories about George's courage, and brought them back to England. As the stories spread, so a popular cult grew up about him.

   You probably associate him with killing a dragon. The story is that he killed a dragon on the flat-topped Dragon Hill at Uffington, Oxfordshire. Legend says that no grass grows where the dragon's blood trickled down.

4. But this could be confusing George with the archangel Michael, who is portrayed in classical pictures wearing armour, with the devil represented as a dragon. In the last book of the Bible, Revelation, Michael and the devil fight, and Michael beats the devil. Down through the ages, various stories have probably got mixed up, eventually giving us the story of George saving a young woman from being eaten by a dragon.

5. It was King Edward III who, in 1350, made George the patron saint of England, and the cult of St George was further advanced by Henry V, at the battle of Agincourt in northern France. William Shakespeare spread the legend further in his play *Henry V*, which features that battle: he used the call 'Cry God for Harry, England and St George!' as Henry's rousing battle call to his troops.

6. So why is George the patron saint of England? The answer to that lies in his reputation as a brave and honourable knight, which is what captured the imagination of the crusaders in the Middle Ages. They modelled themselves on George, fighting for the Christian Church in the Middle East. We find that sort of war difficult to understand now, but we can all respond to a man who refused to deny his faith even under the worst torture.

7. The flag of St George stands for a Christian who was faithful to the point of death. I wonder how many of us could withstand torture rather than deny our faith?

8. In the world today, many people are not free to practise their faith. Governments oppress minority faiths in many countries. One recent example of this was the uprising of Buddhist monks in Burma, who were demonstrating peacefully for the return of democracy to their country. Would you or I have had the faith and strength of those monks to stand up to the military for what we believed in?

9. You may think that you cannot do much to help the world become more accepting of different faiths, and of people's right to practise their faith. One of the easiest things you could do is write letters for Amnesty International. These go either to people who are in prison, to show that the world hasn't forgotten them, or to the governments that are holding them prisoner. Look at the Amnesty website and see how you can join in, and although you won't be tortured like St George, you too can make a real difference.

 Time for reflection

We're going to listen to some music. It is often played when we remember all the military personnel who died during the two World Wars. Perhaps you'd like to think as you listen about how you can help to bring freedom to the world.

You might also like to say a silent prayer for all the people held captive at this time because of their religious belief. (Play 'Nimrod'.)

> *Prayer*
> God of the free, be with all who are suffering for their faith today.
> Help governments and leaders to be open
> and accepting of others who may be different.
> Help me to listen to what other people say,
> and so come to a greater understanding of their beliefs.
> **Amen.**

ST ALBAN
First saint of Britain (22 June)

By Ronni Lamont

Suitable for Key Stage 3

Aim

To look at the life of St Alban and recognize why he is important in our history.

Preparation and materials

- Images of Alban can be found at:
  www.earlybritishkingdoms.com/bios/alban.html
  http://en.wikipedia.org/wiki/Saint_Alban

Assembly

1. Alban was a soldier in the Roman army, around the year 300. He lived and worked in the town that the Romans called Verulamium; the river Ver runs through it. We don't know anything about his background, but we do know that he met an early Christian priest called Amphibalus, and took Amphibalus into his house to save him from persecution and probably death. This was during the time when it was not permitted to be a Christian, and Amphibalus was not only a Christian, but he was a priest, and actively preaching about Jesus. At this time, there were very few Christians in England.

   Alban and Amphibalus were together for long enough for Alban to decide to become a Christian. He was baptized, presumably by night, in the river Ver. Amphibalus taught Alban the Christian faith and they stayed together until the Romans caught wind of where Amphibalus was.

2. When soldiers eventually arrived to arrest Amphibalus, Alban suggested that he and Amphibalus exchange cloaks. So Amphibalus escaped and Alban was arrested. Alban was taken to the Roman governor, who was sacrificing an animal to the local god at the time that Alban was brought in.

When Alban threw back his cloak, the governor realized that this was not Amphibalus. He asked Alban who he was. He is said to have replied: 'I am Alban and I worship and adore the true and living God who created all things.' This was not guaranteeing Alban an easy time.

The governor was so angry that he condemned Alban to death, and here the story has probably been embroidered down through the years ...

3. Alban was led up the hill out of the town towards the execution area, and he had to cross the river. As Alban went into the water, the river dried up. As he walked up the hill, so roses bloomed. When they reached the top, the executioner dropped dead as he tried to decapitate Alban. A second, successful executioner's eye fell out as Alban's head dropped. And on the spot where the head landed, a stream burst up through the eyes.

4. Alban's story became well known, and over time people began to come to worship and remember Alban on the spot where he died. Eventually a shrine was established, and this was gradually enlarged down through the years. Today, in the town that bears the name of St Alban, the cathedral marks this spot, at the top of Holywell Hill.

 Time for reflection

Alban was the first English Christian to die for his faith – the first English martyr, or protomartyr. And while his story is largely unknown, he is remembered through St Albans, a pretty town in Hertfordshire. The cathedral has a shrine, which is said to contain some of his bones.

If you or I were in the same position as Alban – knowing that a friend would die if we didn't act in a very brave and selfless manner, I wonder if we would be able to do what Alban did? For those of us with faith, I wonder if we hold that faith as dear as Alban did?

> *Prayer*
> Lord God of Alban and Amphibalus,
> May we who share their faith
> also share their courage to hold fast to what we believe to be true.
> **Amen.**

Songs

'Who would true valour see?' (*Hymns Ancient and Modern revised*, 293)

'Jesus remember me', Taizé chant (*Hymns Old and New*, 276)

ST BENEDICT
The father of western monasticism (11 July)

By Ronni Lamont

Suitable for Whole School

Aim

To examine the idea of a 'rule of life' for ourselves.

Preparation and materials

- You need to brief the participants. The 'student' sections are suggestions – you may wish to insert others or real heroes of your school in their own fields.

Assembly

1. A student dribbles a football across the space, and then picks up the ball.

   Student: I play for the (*name of school/local club*) football team. We train every week, and I practise at home too. (*Name of local football star*) is my football hero – I'd love to be as good as he is.

2. Another student skateboards across the space, then picks up the skateboard.

   Student: I've been skateboarding for … years. Me and my mates practise in the park most days.

3. Another student walks across the space with a snooker cue.

   Student: I play snooker whenever I have time. Ronnie O'Sullivan is my hero.

4. Two students cross the space speaking French.

   Student: If you don't practise your languages, you're never confident enough to speak to a foreign national. I want to go to Paris in the holidays and be able to order food in French.

5. Finally a student crosses the space, reading from the Bible. (If your school is predominantly another faith, use that faith's holy book and adapt the words accordingly.)

   Student: I'm a Christian. I read my Bible most days so that I can know how God wants me to live my life.

6. If you want to be good at something, we all know you have to practise. You develop what's called a 'rule of life', which helps you to do that in a managed and sensible manner.

7. Benedict was a Roman, born about the year AD 480. When he grew up he was appalled at the life that most Romans were leading, so he left the city and ended up living in a cave for three years while he prayed and thought about his life.

   When the abbot of the local monastery died, the monks came and persuaded Benedict to be their new abbot. But things went so badly wrong that the monks tried to get rid of him by poisoning him, so he left. He eventually set up 12 religious communities in Italy, and in each the monks followed the guidelines that Benedict had devised and lived by.

8. Benedict wrote a book of rules for his followers to live by, and we now know that as the 'Rule of St Benedict'. Many monasteries live by this rule.

   The rule has a unique balance of religious commitment, moderation and reasonableness. Many communities, nuns as well as monks, that were founded in the Middle Ages, decided to follow Benedict's rule.

 Time for reflection

Benedict's rule ensures that those who follow it have a good balance of exercise, prayer and study, as well as work.

How could you make a rule of life that would ensure a good balance of all the elements that you enjoy and know that you need? A balance of food, exercise, work, leisure. Sharing your money with those who have less than you have, being helpful to those in need?

Take a few moments to think about the areas of your life that you give too much time to, and those that maybe need a little more.

Prayer

Help me to bring a healthy balance to the activities and the leisure in my life.

May I always find time for other people, and time for myself. **Amen.**

 Suggested music

'Take this moment' (*Hymns Old and New*, 607)

'Turn turn' by The Byrds (1960s hit single – if you can find it)

ANGELS
St Michael and All Angels
(29 September)

By Paul Hess

Suitable for Whole School

Aim

To enable pupils to see that angels are messengers of God's love for us.

Preparation and materials

- You will need the song 'Angels' by Robbie Williams.
- Bible reading: Genesis 21.17–20.

Assembly

1. Play the song once pupils are settled, rather than as they are coming in – this will give them an opportunity to listen to the words carefully.

2. As a light-hearted introduction, you may wish to conduct a quick poll on the merits of Robbie Williams as a singer, for example: Put your hands up if you are a Robbie fan … if you've even heard of Robbie Williams.

3. Whether you are a Robbie fan or not, there is no denying the power of this particular song. Several years ago it was a huge hit, and it seems to touch something deep within us. Its message goes to the very heart of human existence – the need to be loved completely and unconditionally, the need to be loved and never forsaken.

   (You might like to quote the chorus section that begins: 'And through it all'.)

   Robbie Williams is dreaming of a love that goes beyond human love, a love that is always there, a constant reassuring presence amid all the ups and downs of life.

4. One of the central beliefs of the Christian faith is that God is always there, that the love of God never forsakes us. No matter how bad things get, God's loving presence is always with us –

and, as Robbie Williams' song makes clear, it is angels that remind us of this everlasting, divine love.

5. Now, I hear you say – angels? Great heavenly creatures with large wings and haloes – I've certainly never seen one or I don't believe in them!

It is important to remember that the Greek word *angelos*, from which we get the word angels, simply means 'messenger'. So when we think of angels we should think not only of mighty celestial beings, but of ordinary human messengers – the people in our lives who remind us of God's love for us.

6. It never ceases to amaze me how whenever I am feeling low, someone seems to come along just to ask how I am, to offer a simple word of encouragement or reassurance – or to make me laugh!

(You may wish to insert a simple and personal example of how an 'angel' has helped you in your life.)

It is at moments like this that we are reminded – through other people acting as God's messengers or angels – that God loves us and never forsakes us.

7. When you are going through tough times in life, remember that nothing can separate us from God's love. And remember too – God's angels are closer than you might think …

8. Each one of us is also called to be an angel – to be God's messenger. Each day brings us opportunities to offer friendship and support to those around us – to remind them that they are loved and cared for. Your word of kindness may be exactly what that person needs at that moment.

 Time for reflection

In the book of Genesis we have the story of the slave girl Hagar, who was abandoned in the desert with her son Ishmael. An angel of God comes to remind her that she is not alone.

Read Genesis 21.17–20.

Prayer
Lord, thank you for your angels who remind us that your love never forsakes us.
Help us, too, to be your messengers of love to those around us.
Amen.

I AM LEGEND
Remembrance Day (11 November)

By Helen Redfern

Suitable for Key Stage 4

Aim

To consider what makes a person a legend, in the context of Remembrance Day.

Preparation and materials

- Note that the film *I Am Legend* is certificate 15.
- You might like to play 'Nimrod', from Elgar's *Enigma Variations*, which is often played at Remembrance Day services, as the students enter and leave.

Assembly

1. I wonder who you think of when I say the word 'legend'? Maybe a great footballing legend like George Best? Or a rock legend like Jimi Hendrix? Or a legend of the cinema like John Wayne?

    A person becomes a legend when great stories are told about them long after their death or the height of their fame. Today we will consider three such legends.

2. The film *I Am Legend* is set in the deserted city of New York in 2012. Three years earlier, scientists had discovered what they believed to be a viral cure for cancer, only to find that the side effects caused the destruction of the world as we know it. Dr Robert Neville (played by Will Smith) was one of those scientists.

    Neville chooses to remain in the city as it is evacuated, the only human survivor in an urban wilderness inhabited by wild animals and even wilder mutant humans and dogs. Neville's mission is to reverse the spread of the virus using his own immunity. He chooses to put his own life in danger and to suffer complete isolation in his attempt to rescue humanity.

    He sends out a daily broadcast to any survivors, offering food, shelter and protection, assuring any that may hear: 'Please, you are not alone.'

A young woman and her son come to him with stories of a colony of survivors. The mutants attack the house, just as Neville finds the cure. He gives up his life to protect it. The young woman makes sure that no one ever forgets his sacrifice: 'Dr Robert Neville dedicated his life to the discovery of a cure and the restoration of humanity … We are his legacy. This is his legend.'

He displayed the greatest love of all, laying down his own life for the sake of others.

3. This is how Jesus describes it in John 15.13: 'No one has greater love than this, to lay down one's life for one's friends.'

Christians believe that Jesus came to earth to rescue humanity. Jesus chose to put his own life in danger and to suffer persecution and mocking for the sake of all people. During his life on earth, he assured all who would listen that he would protect and provide for them. He reassured his followers by saying: 'Remember, I am with you always, to the end of the age' (Matthew 28.20).

In the end, Jesus gave his life to save the world. He too displayed the greatest love of all. Over 2,000 years on, many Christians around the world still tell the stories of Jesus and remember his death regularly in services of Holy Communion and every year at Easter time.

4. At this time of year, we remember others who gave their lives for the sake of their country. We do not know all of their names. We do not know all of their stories. But we do know that many have died in wars throughout the centuries to protect us and those who came before us. These men and women have also displayed the greatest love of all, laying down their own lives for their friends, their families, their fellow citizens.

All who have sacrificed their own lives for the sake of others deserve to be remembered.

 Time for reflection

So let us take time to remember all who have died to protect their country and those who live in it.

Let us remember the example that Jesus set in giving his life for the salvation of us all.

Let us think about what we can do today to provide for and protect others who need help at this time.

So let it be.

ST ANDREW
A pattern for life (30 November)

By Ronni Lamont

Suitable for Whole School (Church school)

 Aim

To think about what 'good news' we can share today.

 Preparation and materials

- You will need two readers.

 Assembly

1. One of the readers runs up to the other, and shakes their arm in excitement.

   Reader 1: I've found him, Peter! I've found the one who God promised us all those years ago! The special person, the Messiah!

   Reader 2 (bemused): What? You say you've found the Messiah, the chosen one of God? Where?

   Reader 1: Up by the river! He was watching John baptize people. Come on! Let's go and find him!

   They run off. (Based on John 1.40–42.)

2. Have you ever told someone that something special was going on? That your favourite celebrity was in town? That your favourite band was playing locally? That a certain shop has stocks of the latest must-have gadget? Or even, when you were younger, were you one of those people who shout, 'Fight, fight!' and encourage people to go and watch?

   Those two people we've just seen were excited because Andrew had found someone who they thought was very important, the Messiah, the chosen person God would be sending. He was the person the Jewish people had been waiting and looking for.

3. Andrew told his brother Peter about Jesus, and that's how Peter came to know Jesus. Andrew told Peter, and then Peter told others.

    And in fact we don't know how many people Peter told. Many scholars believe that one of the books that tells the story of Jesus – the Gospel of Mark in the Bible – was based on the sermons and memories of Peter himself.

4. Andrew believed that Jesus was good news. What good news have you heard today? Would any of you like to share some with us all? Take answers, if there are any.

5. All over the world, people will be sharing good news today. Probably not that they've found the Messiah, but perhaps the news of a new baby, of passing an exam, of getting a job. Of getting engaged, or maybe that they love someone.

 Time for reflection

What good news could you share today?

Perhaps you've done all your homework?!

Perhaps you did well in a test?

Perhaps you understand that bit of maths that you've been struggling with?

Perhaps you'd like to tell a friend how much you appreciate them?

Perhaps you'd like to tell a member of your family how much you love them?

What good news could you share today?

> *Prayer*
> Lord, help me to share good news as well as bad.
> Help me to remember the good news of Jesus: that you love us and are there for us.
> And help me to share that good news.
> **Amen.**

 Song

'Go, tell it on the mountain' (*Come and Praise*, 24)

THROUGHOUT THE YEAR

BENDY BITS OF METAL AND RANDOM WORDS
Creativity

By Gordon Lamont

Suitable for Key Stages 3 and 4

Aim

To consider the amazing creative potential of the human mind.

Preparation and materials

- You will need a handful of paperclips and a dictionary.
- The ideas in this assembly are taken from *The Confidence Book* (Gordon Lamont, Sheldon Press, 2007).
- See:
  www.assemblies.org.uk/2006/jul06sec_creativethinking.php
  for another assembly idea on this theme.

Assembly

1. Hand out some paperclips to a selection of students and say that you are going to give them all just 30 seconds to come up with uses for 'this object' – don't refer to it as a paperclip. Ask the students to pass the objects around so that others have a chance to 'play' with them.

2. At the end of the 30 seconds ask for suggestions: What ideas have you come up with for using this object?

    Value all ideas – you might need to be ready for some of the less hygienic ones! If ideas are slow to come, point out that you saw several people bending the objects about so that's one use: an executive desk toy, even a stress reliever!

    Other ideas might include: a small ruler; a TV aerial for a doll's house; a stencil; a fingernail cleaner; emergency clothes fastening; and even … something for holding papers together!

3. Point out that you avoided giving the object a name because once we give things names we think of them in a certain way – call it a paperclip and that's all it is.

   Suggest to the students that they can use this 'seeing things differently' approach with any problem. Allow yourself to see things in a different way and maybe you'll find a way forward.

4. Choose one of the suggestions for what to do with the 'paperclip'. Produce your dictionary and explain that the human mind has a seemingly infinite ability to make connections and create stories – and you're all going to do that now. The starting point is the chosen use of the paperclip; the next element will be generated at random using the dictionary.

   Ask one student to open the dictionary at random and another student to point, without looking, at any word, then read it out – if necessary, including the definition.

5. Ask for suggestions – who can make a story link between your object and the word you've just generated?

   Take one suggestion and then generate another random word and feed this into the story. Point out that this is an excellent technique for when you get stuck with writing – generate a random word and see where it takes you.

 Time for reflection

The human mind is amazing.

We make connections all the time. We're always on the look-out for something new.

How will you use your creativity today?

> *Prayer*
> Thank you for the creative spark within us all.
> Thank you for stories, for connections, for fresh thoughts and new ideas.
> Help me to use my creativity every day and in every way that I can.
> **Amen.**

DOES SIZE MATTER?
People look at the outside, but God looks at the heart

By Oliver Harrison

Suitable for Key Stage 3 (Church school)

Aim

To talk about good things coming in small packages, to show that size can be deceptive.

Preparation and materials

- You will need an LP (12-inch vinyl), a CD, and an MP3 player.
- Bible reading: 1 Samuel 16.1–13.

Assembly

1. Show the LP. Ask if the students know what it is! Explain and talk about it. Say that it can hold about 40 minutes of music.

   Show the CD. Ask the students what it is, and explain and talk about it. Say that it can hold about 80 minutes of music. Twice as much and yet it's smaller.

   Show the MP3 player. Ask how many of the students have one in their pocket right now? How much music can yours hold?

   It's the smallest of the three but it can hold the most music. The music running time is the equivalent of a whole school week: you could start it on a Monday morning and play it every day and every night all week until Friday.

2. Talk about good things coming in small packages, and that size can be deceptive. For example, bank notes are all about the same size …

3. There's a story in the Bible (1 Samuel 16.1–13) about how God sees people.

   King Saul wasn't a very good king in God's eyes. God decided to send Samuel, the prophet, who spoke for God, to appoint the next king.

When Samuel arrived at the town of Bethlehem, God told him to go to the home of a man called Jesse. Jesse had many sons, and Samuel asked to see them all. They came in descending age order. The eldest was fully grown, an adult who served in the army. Samuel assumed that God meant that this son must be the new king, but God said no. In Samuel's heart he felt God saying: 'People look at the outside, but I look at the heart.'

So the next young man came in, and the next, and the next. After seven sons had come in, and God had said no to all of them, Samuel asked Jesse if he had any more sons. Jesse admitted that he did: the youngest, David, who was still a boy, was keeping the sheep out on the hills. Samuel looked at David when he arrived, and knew that he was God's choice for king. God liked the way David thought and acted. God liked his heart. (Although you might like to know that the writer of the story also tells us how good-looking David was – somewhat spoiling the moral of the story!)

4. The Bible says that God does not judge by appearances but by the heart; not by how big or pretty or handsome or fit or strong someone is on the outside but by what they are like on the inside: are they kind and honest and wise? And are they people, as King David would be, who when they make mistakes are courageous enough to say sorry, and start again?

 Time for reflection

Think about the people who you consider to be attractive.

They might be a celebrity,
they might be your friend,
they might be a sports star.

Now think about the people who you like to be with.
People you trust,
people who care for you,
people with good hearts.

Prayer
People look at the outside, but God looks at the heart.
May my heart be good, and acceptable.
Amen.

LOOKING FORWARDS AND LOOKING BACKWARDS
New year

By Helen Levesley

Suitable for Whole School

Aim

To identify the positive in both the past and the future.

Preparation and materials

- You will need an image of the ancient Roman god Janus. See: http://images.google.co.uk/images?hl=en&q=Janus&btnG=Search+Images&gbv=2 (the recommended one is that from the Vatican).

Assembly

1. What do you see in this picture? The faces of two people? One looking forwards and one looking backwards? This is the Roman god Janus. He was the god of beginnings and endings and his image appeared on gates, doors, doorways.

2. Beginnings and endings is the theme for our assembly today. We have just begun a new year, and seen out the old one. No doubt you had a great time! However, beginning something new, and coming to the end of something, can bring us a time for reflection and thinking about what has passed.

3. Let's think about endings. Whether it is the ending of a great film that you really enjoyed, or the end of a cup of tea, or even the end of someone's life: these are things that we can all associate with. Think about the feelings associated with endings: sadness, disappointment and a sense of deflation.

   However, endings can be a good thing too. The end of an exam, the end of a boring lesson; and for some people, death can mean the end of a long and painful illness. Endings are times when we feel that something has changed, and probably will not be the same again.

4. Look back over the year that has just gone. One that we will never have again (a scary thought in itself). How was it for you? Was it a good year full of fulfilled promise and excitement or was it a really difficult year with many challenges? I guess for most of you there was a mixture of good and bad.

    The start of a new year is an excellent chance for us to look back over the year just gone. What could we have done better? How could things have been changed? What could I have done to make things different? We know that we cannot remain in the past – people and things that do that never move on, and are left behind.

5. Instead, let us look now to the future, like our double-headed god Janus, whose name incidentally is the reason we are now in the month of January. A time for looking back, and also for looking forward. For we are now standing on the threshold of a new, and exciting year.

    Look ahead now to the new year and all the possibilities and opportunities it holds. For some of you, your GCSEs, for others going away to university, or major life events such as marriage or having children. There are so many possibilities.

    We hold this year in the palm of our hands – we have in our control the things that often cause us regret when we look back: the way we did or did not behave; how we are with others. This new year could, when you look back on it in a couple of years' time, be your best year ever. I really hope for us all that it is.

 Time for reflection

Prayer
When I look back, allow me to see the positive in my actions
rather than to be sad at what I have left undone.
Let me be able to see where I could have done better,
but also to look back and reflect on what brought me to that
    place.

As I look forward, allow me to be positive,
to see that the new year is all before me,
and that what I do makes a difference.

Whether it is looking forwards to the future or back to the past, give me the strength to go on.
Amen.

 Song

'One more step' (*Come and Praise*, 47)

FOUR MINUTES
Don't take life for granted

By Helen Redfern

Suitable for Whole School

Aim

To explore the question: What would you do if you knew you had only four minutes to live?

Preparation and materials

- Download the song 'Four Minute Warning' by Mark Owen.
- Bible reading: Luke 12.16–21.

Assembly

1. What do you think of when I say 'four minutes'? The time it will take for this assembly to be over? The song by Madonna and Justin Timberlake? The length of time you spent in the shower this morning? The first four-minute mile run by Roger Bannister?

   If you asked a teacher, parent or grandparent, they may give you a very different answer.

2. Between 1953 and 1992, the Cold War existed between the West and the Soviet Union. Britain felt the real threat of a Soviet nuclear attack throughout that period. The four-minute warning was a public alert system conceived by the British government to notify the population of such an attack. It was believed that Soviet nuclear missiles once launched would take four minutes to reach their target. During that time, it was important to take cover and follow certain procedures.

   Many people considered how they would spend their final four minutes. Telling friends and family how much they loved them? Playing their guitar for the last time? Listening to a favourite track? Cuddling their beloved pet?

   It's an interesting question to ask. How would you spend the last four minutes of your life? (*Pause for a moment of reflection.*)

It has occupied the minds of several generations and been the subject of numerous songs and books, including Mark Owen's song 'Four Minute Warning' released in 2003.

3. However, with the end of the Cold War, the nuclear danger is no longer in the forefront of people's minds. The threat of imminent death has disappeared from the consciousness of the people. You might say that some people believe they can live for ever. They take life for granted.

In the Bible, Jesus tells the story of a man who had not given death a single thought (Luke 12.16–21). He was rich and successful, because his land had produced abundant crops. He had to build bigger and bigger barns to store the crops. When he had done this, he said to himself: 'Relax, eat, drink, be merry' (12.19). But God said to him, 'You fool! This very night your life is being demanded of you' (12.20).

4. None of us knows the year, the day, the hour when our lives will be over. It could be an accident, an illness, a terrorist attack, a heroic act … one thing is for sure, we will all die. Some people try to live each day as if it will be their last, never going to bed without resolving conflicts or making good relationships that might have been tough that day.

Is this something you could attempt? Life is not just about living for now; life is not lived just to relax, eat, drink and be merry. It is also good to take the time to reflect on how to live in the knowledge that one day, we will die.

 Time for reflection

Let us reflect again on the four-minute warning. How would you spend your final four minutes?

Your answer reveals the things and the people that you really care about.

Sometimes our possessions and ambitions can get in the way of what matters most in our lives.

As you listen to the song (Mark Owen's 'Four Minute Warning', or some other suitable reflective music):

Be thankful for your life and the people that you care about.

Be reminded of what is really important to you.

Be determined never to take what matters most for granted.

INTERNATIONAL DAY OF PEACE
World Peace Day (21 September)

By James Lamont

Suitable for Key Stages 4 and 5

 Aim

To look at the concept of World Peace Day.

 Preparation and materials

- Download pictures taken from news sites showing people suffering through war. Include some of UN peacekeeping forces.
- You need a copy of 'Nimrod' from the *Enigma Variations* by Elgar.

 Assembly

1. We live in a world where peace is elusive. Despite the existence of peacemaking organizations, such as the United Nations, and a public dislike of war, the UN's peacekeeping forces are, at the time of writing, deployed in 16 separate missions across the globe. Nations as diverse as Lebanon, Haiti, Cyprus and India host international forces, determined to control and extinguish local and sometimes widespread conflicts. Yet, for one day, on 21 September each year, a day-long ceasefire is called for, to remind the world of the value of peace and the difficulty of maintaining it.

2. Since 1981, the Peace Bell has been rung at UN headquarters in New York on this day. The bell is made from coins donated by children from across the globe. It was given to the UN as a gift from Japan, a country that turned its back on armed conflict after World War Two and has emerged as one of the world's strongest economies and a major international player. The bell is inscribed with the words 'Long Live Absolute World Peace'.

3. World peace is a noble goal in the abstract, but is peace itself the real goal? Following World War Two, after liberation from the Nazi threat, the citizens of the former Soviet Union found themselves living under a different kind of tyranny. Peace was achieved but at the price of the freedom of the people living under communism.

4. In 2004, the UN planned to release a set of stamps to commemorate World Peace Day. One of the winning designs was by Yang Chih-yuan, a student from Taiwan. Taiwan is an island nation off the coast of mainland China and is populated by Chinese people. However, it regards itself as a separate country and has its own government and cultural identity. Because China does not recognize Taiwan as a sovereign nation, it stopped the UN from producing the stamp.

5. There was, however, a happy ending. Following discussion at the UN, the stamp was released across the world. What this shows, though, is that, in our world, the demand for peace is often used as a mask to perpetuate injustice and the rule of the strong. Until the hungry are fed and the just rewarded, we will always live under the shadow of war. With one billion people in the world going hungry, the need for true peace has never been so vital, as peace without justice is just an extension of war.

 Time for reflection

Play 'Nimrod' and show the pictures of people suffering.

Peace, perfect peace …
Hope in despair
Light in the darkness
How long, Lord, how long?

Love, perfect love …
Joy in pain
Light in the darkness
How long, Lord, how long?

Peace, perfect peace …
Coming to all
With me bringing it in
Light in the darkness
How long, Lord, how long?

Prayer
Lord, bring peace to our troubled world:
peace that is just,
peace that is fair,
peace for all.
Amen.

 Song

'For the healing of the nations' (*Hymns Old and New*, 139)

LOOK AT WHAT I'VE MADE!
Creativity

By Helen Redfern

Suitable for Whole School

 Aim

To value creativity in ourselves and others, and in the One who created us.

 Preparation and materials

- You will need a fresh flower; something that you have made at some stage in your life; a young child's picture; an exercise book; a paintbrush.
- You might also like to download pictures of some of the items mentioned below, such as Van Gogh's *Sunflowers*.

 Assembly

1. Who created:

- *The Simpsons*? (Matt Groening)
- *Sunflowers* painting? (Van Gogh)
- *The Angel of the North*? (Anthony Gormley)
- St Paul's Cathedral? (Sir Christopher Wren)
- 'Patience', 'Shine' and 'Rule the World'? (Take That) (or you might like to choose a different trio of tracks if Take That are a bit passé for your students)
- *Macbeth*? (William Shakespeare)
- The formula $E=mc^2$? (Albert Einstein)
- The miniskirt? (Mary Quant)
- A beautiful flower? (Show your real flower and see what responses you get.)
- This? (Produce something you have made and see if anyone can guess that you made it!)

2. Take the object you made and elaborate on it. How old were you when you made it? Why did you make it? Who was it for? How did you feel when you had finished it?

We have all made things. Maybe not masterpieces like Van Gogh and Shakespeare, but we have all made things that we are proud of. We are all creative in our own way.

3. Listen to this account of something the writer made when he was a child:

When I was five, my family visited my grandparents in California during Christmas vacation. They lived in an apartment building with an alley beside it – very exciting for a boy who lived on a farm in Michigan. At some point in my exploration of the alley, I decided to make a Christmas present for my dad out of the things I found there. So on the morning of the twenty-fifth, my father had the privilege of opening a gift of a piece of black and green drainpipe glued to a flat grey rock with little white stones resting on the inside of it.

A masterpiece, to say the least.

The reason I remember this is because I visited my dad at his office a few days ago, and while I waited for him to finish his meeting, I wandered around looking at the pictures on his walls and the papers on his desk and the things on his shelves. On one of his shelves sat the drainpipe and rock sculpture, thirty years later.

He still has it.

He brought it home with him and put it in his office in 1977 and hasn't gotten rid of it.

We know why he kept it. How you treat the creation reflects how you feel about the creator.

From Sex God *by Rob Bell, Zondervan, 2007, pp. 27–8, used by permission of Zondervan*

4. How you treat the creation reflects how you feel about the creator. Think about that.

Ever written a poem for a girl and been asked, 'Is that the best you can do?' (*Look in the exercise book and discard it.*)

Ever been given a picture by a younger brother and screwed it up and thrown it in the bin? (*Look at the picture and then screw it up.*)

Ever tried really hard to paint a good picture and been told, 'Stick to the day job'? (*Pretend to be painting.*)

Ever whispered to a friend in hymn practice, 'You call that singing?'

5. How others treat what we have made affects us. What others say about what we have made matters to us. In the same way, how we treat what others have made affects them. What we say about what others have made matters to them.

 Time for reflection

(*Hold up the flower.*)

And who made this beautiful flower?

Who made the stars and rivers and trees?

Who made the whole earth and everything in it?

Many people believe that God created the world and all that lives in it. It says in Genesis that 'God saw everything that he had made, and indeed, it was very good' (Genesis 1.31).

Very good? Absolutely amazing, I would say! No one in the whole of history has ever come close to creating what God has created!

Let us spend a moment thinking about the beautiful things in the world around us.

And let's remember: How you treat the creation reflects how you feel about the creator:

Destruction of the rain forests ...
Pollution of the seas ...
Extinction of hunted animal species ...
How you treat the creation reflects how you feel about the creator.

Broken glass in parks ...
Rubbish littering the streets ...
Graffiti on walls ...
How you treat the creation reflects how you feel about the creator.

Refusing to help those who need it ...
Laughing at those who are different from you ...
Hurting others by what you say and do ...
How you treat the creation reflects how you feel about the creator.

Prayer
Creator God, we thank you for all that you have made.
We are sorry when we do not look after your creation as we
    should.
Help us to help you make the world a better place.
Amen.

 Suggested songs and music

'Jesus is Lord! Creation's voice proclaims it' (*Hymns Old and New*, 270)

'All things bright and beautiful' (*Hymns Old and New*, 21)

'All creatures of our God and King' (*Hymns Old and New*, 9)

'For the beauty of the earth' (*Hymns Old and New*, 137)

'Almighty God' (Tim Hughes)

'What a wonderful world' (Louis Armstrong)

'NOT WAVING BUT DROWNING'
Sharing your deepest secrets

By Paul Hess

Suitable for Whole School

Aim

To enable students to understand that it is important to share our deepest feelings.

Preparation and materials

- You may wish to play and quote from the song 'Nobody Knows', by The Toni Rich Project, as an introduction to the assembly (or you could use Smokey Robinson's 'The Tracks of my Tears'). The lyrics to both songs (available online) illustrate very well the theme of the assembly: the veneer we construct to hide our true feelings.
- You will need the poem 'Not Waving But Drowning' by Stevie Smith.

Assembly

1. Read out the poem 'Not Waving But Drowning' by Stevie Smith.

2. On numerous occasions today – 10, 15, 20 – you and I will be asked how we are by someone we encounter in or out of school. On nearly all those occasions, we will utter a standard response: 'I'm fine', I'm cool'. And of course most of the time that is entirely the appropriate response. When an acquaintance asks you 'All right?' as they pass you in the corridor on the way to third period, it is not generally the time to say, 'Well no, actually I feel overpowered by a black cloud of depression and I just don't see the point of existence'!

3. But all of us *do* need a space, a safe place, where we can be ourselves and where we can be honest about how we really feel. Such a place may be with your family or with a close friend. It may be that you need to find such a place with the school counsellor. (*There is an opportunity here to advertise the school counsellor or whatever other confidential pastoral services your school offers.*)

Whoever we confide in, all of us need a place where we don't have to wear a mask or play a role – where we don't have to act the clown or the joker, or the hip-hop gangsta or the hard rugby lad or the ultra-chic supermodel.

4. Very often we create these personas to protect ourselves – both from other people and from the pain inside ourselves. In doing so, we can become like the person in Stevie Smith's poem: someone who gives the impression of being fine, someone who is 'waving' ('yeah, I'm fine, no problem') when they are actually drowning; that is, when you are feeling unhappy, depressed or anxious. If we continually pretend everything is fine when it is not, we risk becoming isolated and alone – and ultimately we will be unable to cope with all the demands and pressures of life.

5. At the heart of the Christian faith, indeed, at its very beginning, is the idea of the God who created us, and thus who knows us better than we know ourselves. Christians believe that it is in their relationship with God that they can truly be themselves. In prayer we don't have to wear a mask or pretend – we can be totally honest and open. When we are with God, we can admit to being vulnerable.

May each of us find, in our relationship with God and our relationships with other people, a place where we can truly be ourselves, where we can be totally honest.

 Time for reflection

O LORD, you have searched me and known me.
You know when I sit down and when I rise up;
  you discern my thoughts from far away.
You search out my path and my lying down,
  and are acquainted with all my ways.

Psalm 139.1–3

Prayer
Lord, you know us better than we know ourselves:
give us the grace to acknowledge our weakness and vulnerability.
Thank you that although sometimes we feel alone, you are always
  with us.
Amen.

ON THE BIG ISSUE
Homelessness

By James Lamont

Suitable for Key Stages 4 and 5

Aim

To look at one answer to the problem of homelessness and begging.

Preparation and materials

- Music: 'Don't Judge Me' by Sting or 'Another Day in Paradise' by Phil Collins (both available online).

Assembly

1. Homes take many forms: flats, houses, maisonettes, bungalows, houseboats, trailers, etc. There are two things that all of these share: first, they are structures designed to protect their inhabitants against the weather, the cold and the rain, which can be dangerous if one is exposed to them for too long. Second, they fulfil a psychological need that we have for a sense of home, somewhere we belong.

2. Imagine that you are staying at a friend's house. It's fun for the first night, good for the second, but by the twelfth night you are feeling uncomfortable as it's not your own space. The need for one's own environment is well recognized by psychologists and social scientists.

3. Imagine, then, that everything about your home environment is taken away from you. You are left out in the street, surrounded by other people's homes, without one yourself. You have to sleep where you can, trying to balance safety with warmth and shelter. People walk past you; they do not see you as you, only as a beggar, a homeless person: one who has slipped through a crack in society, a crack that can be a one-way trip. Alcoholism, drug addiction and mental illness, as well as a hostile populace, are factors driving people onto the streets and keeping them there.

4. How can one make a living in such a circumstance? The most common means is begging. The problems with this are many. Begging can never be a sustainable job: you cannot beg your way out of begging. Begging can provide a meal for the night and a bus ticket, but it cannot pay for much more.

5. In 1991 John Bird and Gordon Roddick founded *The Big Issue*, as a response to these challenges. This initiative allows the homeless to sell a magazine to people in the street. The magazine currently retails for £1.50 and is supplied to the vendor at a price of 70p a copy. Thus, the vendor receives 80p per magazine sold. This can provide a reasonable income, especially for someone with no mortgage or rent, and no tax to pay. However, it offers more: by providing homeless people with a job and their own income, it also grants dignity to those who are especially vulnerable. Prominent vendors often become minor local celebrities, raising awareness of the plight of the homeless.

6. Some people have criticized the venture, arguing that it fails to deal with substance abuse and alcoholism, which in some cases are the causes, and not the effects, of homelessness. In 1995 The Big Issue Foundation was launched, which provides additional aid to the homeless. Funded by private donations as well as by profits from magazine sales, it investigates and aims to improve the situations that lead to homelessness in the first place.

7. While these measures will not eliminate homelessness and street poverty, it is certainly true that they bring a marked improvement to individual lives and that is no bad thing. The wider changes needed to solve these problems once and for all can only be achieved by huge numbers of people working together. It is important to raise the quality of life for a few, but we should never lose sight of the bigger picture as well.

 Time for reflection

Play one of the songs. You might like to project some of the words up as you listen.

Imagine you are homeless.

How would you feel?

How would you cope?

Think about *The Big Issue* vendors who you might have seen.

Have you ever bought a copy? Did you talk with the vendor? Or did you not even look at them?

Be quietly thankful for all that you have in your life.

> *Prayer*
> You might like to think quietly about your homes, and be thankful.
> **Amen.**

'ONE MAN COME IN THE NAME OF LOVE'
The difference one person can make

By Paul Hess

Suitable for Key Stages 4 and 5

Aim

To enable pupils to understand that one person acting in a good and just cause can make a substantial difference to the world.

Preparation and materials

- You will need a recording of the U2 song 'Pride (In the Name of Love)', which can be found on *U2 The Best of 1980–1990*. Either play it as pupils enter, or start the assembly by playing the song once students are seated. The words of the song could be displayed.
- If possible, display the photograph of the Tiananmen Square 'tank man' – many are available on Google Images and other places on the internet.
- Images of the other figures mentioned in the assembly – Martin Luther King, Rosa Parks and Gandhi – are freely available and would further enhance the presentation.

Assembly

1. Play the U2 song 'Pride'. This song was written in honour of Dr Martin Luther King (it mentions 4 April, this being the day of his murder). The point of the song is that while an assassin's bullet ended his life, it could not end his vision, the identity he had shaped for black and white Americans. In this song U2 are saying that the power of love, a power embodied in the life of Martin Luther King, is far greater than the might of weapons, oppression and hatred. Dr King was 'one man come in the name of love'.

2. The protests led by Martin Luther King were initiated by the actions of another courageous person, Rosa Parks. Rosa was an ordinary black woman living in the highly segregated town of Montgomery in America. One day in 1955 as she was travelling

on a crowded bus she was ordered to stand up so that white passengers could sit down. Tired of the humiliations inflicted on the black community over the years, she refused. The conductor was staggered by her defiance and she was arrested. Her actions led to the Montgomery bus boycott, which in turn acted as a springboard for the whole civil rights struggle. Rosa Parks was 'one woman come in the name of love'.

3. On 5 June 1989 the tanks of the Chinese army rolled ominously into Tiananmen Square in Beijing. Their goal was to crush the pro-democracy demonstrations by students and other activists, which had been breaking out throughout China in the spring of that year.

   Suddenly, to the amazement of all around, one man emerged from the crowd – and stood directly in front of one of the tanks! One ordinary man stopped the might of the feared Chinese army! When the tank tried to go round him he moved to block it. Eventually, he climbed on to the tank to talk to the driver. No one knows for sure what happened to the man who has become known as the 'tank man', but his action showed the power of the human spirit to resist tyranny. He was 'one man come in the name of love'.

4. This too was the power of Mahatma Gandhi – the humble man in peasant's clothes who brought the mighty British Empire to its knees, armed only with the weapons of love, peace and justice. Gandhi believed passionately that if his cause was a just one he would win – no matter how powerful were the forces against him. He famously said: 'Even if you are a minority of one, the truth is the truth.' Gandhi was 'one man come in the name of love'.

5. At the heart of the Christian faith there is also 'one man come in the name of love'. When Jesus comes to Jerusalem days before his death, he knows that it is there that he will come into conflict with the might of the Roman Empire and with the fury of the Jewish religious establishment. And so he comes armed – armed with the weapons of love, forgiveness and peace. He comes riding the humble donkey.

6. Into a world of division and barbarism and violence – a world, in other words, not unlike our own – comes the Prince of Peace, whose power lies not in military might, but in selfless love. And here's the thing: his kingdom, established by the power of love,

rather than bullets, has lasted far longer and been far more influential than the kingdom of any military conqueror.

 Time for reflection

What are you and I prepared to do in the name of love? Do we have even a fraction of the courage of the tank man, or Rosa Parks, or Martin Luther King, or Gandhi? Can we walk with Jesus in the way of the cross?

In the face of a world of greed, violence and oppression, here at school in the face of the bully and the aggressor or in the face of those who simply do not care – what will you and I do in the name of love?

Prayer
Lord, give us vision that we may see a better world,
and give us courage that we may act to make it happen.
Amen.

 Suggested music

'Christ's is the world' (*Hymns Old and New*, 83)

The U2 song could be played as the students leave.

ORDINARY PEOPLE
Confronting prejudice

By Helen Redfern

Suitable for Whole School

Aim

To show that ordinary people can speak out against injustice and make a difference.

Preparation and materials

- If possible, a projected picture of each person as they are introduced would add to the presentation:
  Martin Luther King:
  www.bbc.co.uk/history/historic_figures/king_martin_luther.shtml
  www.bbc.co.uk/radio4/history/sceptred_isle/page/226.shtml?question=226
  Rosa Parks: www.spartacus.schoolnet.co.uk/USAparksR.htm
  Hairspray: www.imdb.com/title/tt0427327/plotsummary

Assembly

1. Can you imagine a time when black people were only allowed to sit on certain seats at the back of a bus? When black people were not allowed to vote in elections? Can you imagine a town where black and white children had to attend separate schools? Where black and white young people were separated at dances by a line down the middle of the room?

2. Fifty years ago, in the southern states in America, this was how it was. Let's hear about three ordinary people who had the courage to speak out.

3. An ordinary clergyman, with a minister for a father and a teacher for a mother, organized peaceful protests and boycotts against discrimination. Here was an ordinary black man who spoke out against the injustice that he saw. This ordinary black man delivered extraordinary speeches with memorable lines such as 'I have a dream that one day down in Alabama ... little black boys

and black girls will be able to join hands with little white boys and white girls as sisters and brothers.'

This man was Martin Luther King, Nobel Peace Prize winner in 1964, assassinated in 1968 when just 39 years old.

4. In the town of Montgomery, like most places in the deep south, buses were segregated. On 1 December 1955, Rosa Parks left Montgomery Fair, the department store where she worked, and got on the bus that she caught every night. As always, she sat in the 'black section' at the back of the bus. However, when the bus became full, the driver instructed Rosa to give up her seat to a white person. When she refused, she was arrested by the police.

In protest against bus segregation, it was decided that from 5 December, black people in Montgomery would refuse to use the buses until passengers were completely integrated. For 382 days, the 17,000 black people in Montgomery walked to work. Eventually, the loss of revenue and a decision by the Supreme Court forced the Montgomery Bus Company to accept integration.

An ordinary woman showed extraordinary courage. This ordinary woman became known as the 'Mother of the Civil Rights Movement'.

5. Those two examples are completely true. This one is not. It is taken from the 2007 hit movie *Hairspray*. It's Baltimore, 1962, and Tracy Turnblad, an ordinary young girl, is obsessed with the Corny Collins Show. Tracy auditions for the show and gets to appear – a dream come true! However, she becomes aware of the way that her black dancer friends are being treated and realizes that she has to do something. As she tells her father, 'I think I've kind of been in a bubble … thinking that fairness was gonna just happen. It's not. People like me are gonna have to get up off their fathers' laps and go out and fight for it.' This ordinary young girl brings about an extraordinary integration.

 Time for reflection

Who will speak out against child labour?
Who will take a stand against bullying?
Who will stand up and challenge racism?
Who will speak for those who have no voice?

(*Pause*)

Not me, that's for sure.
Who would listen to me?
There's nothing special about me.
Nothing I say would make any difference.

(*Pause*)

We are all ordinary people.
Fairness is not going to just happen.
Ordinary people need to find their voice.
Take a stand. Speak out. Make a difference.
Today.

Suggested songs and music

'You Can't Stop the Beat!' (original soundtrack from the film *Hairspray*)

'Almighty Father, who dost give' (*Hymns Ancient and Modern Revised*, 583)

'For the healing of the nations' (*Hymns Old and New*, 139)

'The right hand of God is writing in our land' (www.familyfriendly churches.org.uk/midihymns)

'Make me a channel of your peace' (*Hymns Old and New*, 328)

PLEASE CALL MY NAME!
Each of us is called by God

By Paul Hess

Suitable for Whole School

Aim

To enable students to understand that each one of us has a personal and unique calling from God.

Preparation and materials

- You may wish to replace the story (or the football team!) with one of your own. Any story that involves the disappointment of your name not being called (e.g. not being successful in an audition, a trial, a job interview, etc.) would be suitable.
- Bible reading: Matthew 22.1–10.

Assembly

1. Like so many boys of his age, Joe's great dream was to become a professional footballer and don the claret and blue of mighty West Ham! He played his heart out for his club – and one day he got his big break. He was invited to the under-14 county trials. Yet when the day came Joe was so nervous that he couldn't play his best football. The ball got stuck under his feet and the opposing defenders easily pushed him off the ball.

   At the end of the session the coach read out the list of names of those boys to be invited back. Joe feared the worst, but was hoping against hope … *Please call my name, please call my name,* he said to himself. The coach began reading the names: 'Michael, Ed, Mark' (*for some comic and dramatic effect, you might read the names of pupils in the school at this point*).

   The coach started folding up his piece of paper – he had clearly come to the last name. Joe held his breath.

   'And the final person we'd like to come back for the second trial is … Tom!'

Joe was devastated. The consoling words of his parents had no effect on him on the journey home as the tears welled up. How he had prayed that his name would be called!

2. For each one of us it may be hugely important for our name to be called, for us to be recognized and acknowledged, to feel that we are somebody. We want to feel part of the team. When we are called by name ('Joe, Kate, Ollie – come and be part of our group'), it feels good, we feel as if we belong.

3. And in the same way, when our name is not called, when we are left out, when nobody calls us, we can feel lonely and alienated – it can feel as if we don't fit in, as if no one really cares. Sometimes, if we feel like that for long enough, we might even resort to being disruptive, at the back of the classroom or at home – just so that our names will be called. Poor behaviour is a pretty sure-fire way to get noticed!

4. At the very heart of the biblical message, at the very beginning of the story of faith, lies the 'call' of God. God calls Abraham to establish his people. God calls Moses to set his people free. God calls Paul to spread the gospel. And God calls each of them by name.

But their dramatic callings simply serve to underline the truth that we are *all* called – each one of us. One of the most powerful images in the Bible is the wedding banquet – that God's kingdom is like a feast, a party, and we are all invited, we are all called.

5. Not many of us (sadly) have a calling to become a professional footballer. But we are all called to belong to God's family. We are called to some special task, to do something that will make the world a better place.

6. But you have never heard the call, I hear you say – you have never had a dramatic experience like Moses or Paul. The point is that we must learn to *listen*. God speaks through other people, through circumstances, and most of all God speaks through the language of silence.

If only we could learn to listen, we would hear God's call to each one of us. We would find the special task that is ours to do.

Time for reflection

'I have prepared my dinner, my oxen and my fat calves have been slaughtered, and everything is ready; come to the wedding banquet' (Matthew 22.4).

(You may wish to read the whole of Matthew 22.1–10.)

Prayer
Lord, open our ears, that we may hear your voice,
and open our hearts, that we may respond to your call.
Amen.

Song

'I, the Lord of sea and sky' (*Hymns Old and New*, 235)

REAPING AND SOWING
Working for success

By Brian Radcliffe

Suitable for Whole School

Aim

Students are encouraged to consider the way that academic achievements are based on careful preparation.

Preparation and materials

- You will need a variety of seasonal fresh fruit and vegetables.

Assembly

1. In the agricultural communities of the northern hemisphere this is harvest time. Indicate the display of fruit and veg. Fruit, vegetables and grain crops will be cut and stored for the winter ahead. There will be singing, dancing, eating and drinking because the season has been a success and there's little chance of starvation through the winter.

    (Pause)

2. At least that's how it used to be, before the invention of the fridge and freezer, before crops were chilled and airlifted across the globe so we could have strawberries and grapes in January, parsnips and sprouts in July. That's how it used to be before canning and processing enabled us to stockpile fish and meat to consume at our leisure.

    (Pause)

3. So what's the point of remembering the harvest? I think there are two reasons why it's useful to continue with harvest traditions.

    The first is about contentment. We're bombarded daily with advertising that aims to make us discontent. We're offered new and exciting products to make us look better, feel better and enjoy our life more. We're given the impression that our life as it is now is lacking some vital ingredient. We're persuaded to feel discontented. Harvest encourages us to stop and count what is good and satisfying in our lives. It encourages us to focus on what we have rather than on what we don't have. It starts with the plentiful supply of food and drink in the shops and then encourages us to widen our focus to take in the technology, the people, the opportunities that surround us. Harvest encourages contentment.

4. The second reason for continuing with harvest traditions is because it reminds us of the way that life is a continuous process. The quality of the harvest depends on what has been done earlier. The ground will need preparation: ploughing and fertilizing of the fields creates a suitable environment into which the best-quality seed is planted. Careful weeding, watering and feeding encourage the germination and growth of the seeds into young plants. Sunshine and warm weather help the fruit and seeds to ripen ready for harvesting.

5. Jesus used the image of this process to teach about ways to live our lives. He talked about the way the same seed can produce a different harvest, depending on the quality of the soil into which it's planted. He suggested that this was like the way we respond differently to the advice and teaching we're given. We might ignore it, forget it, become discouraged by it or benefit from it. He talked about the way an unfriendly neighbour might throw some weed seeds into our carefully prepared beds, reminding us of the way other people can distract us from our targets. He talked of the way that a grape vine needs to be pruned in order to encourage a good crop, showing that some sacrifice might be necessary if we are to reach our full potential.

6. In school, September – the harvest month – is the start of the process, at least in educational terms. It's now that we can get the work/leisure/life balance right, guard against distractions, which could be people or other activities, and organize ourselves to meet the deadlines that we're going to face. Maybe we even need to make some short-term sacrifices to make a long-term gain. If we prepare correctly now, and this school plants the best-quality seeds of learning, which I'm sure we will, then hopefully next summer there'll be some impressive results, the consequences of your preparations. It'll be a harvest worth celebrating.

Time for reflection

Spend a moment considering the following thoughts. You may wish to turn them into a prayer:

Be thankful for the opportunities for success in sport, performance, academic subjects and any other aspect of school life that you enjoy.

Be sorry for the failures over the past year that happened because you didn't do the right preparation.

Make a plan to take some action that arises out of today's assembly. Have the courage to do something that will make a difference.

Suggested music

Play the track 'Harvest for the World' by The Christians.

SECRET LIVES
What's going on in other people's lives?

By Brian Radcliffe

Suitable for Whole School

Aim

Students are encouraged to consider their own sensitivity to what might be happening in one another's lives.

Preparation and materials

None required.

Assembly

1. It's a sad yet often interesting task to clear the house belonging to an elderly person who has recently died. You never know quite what you may unearth.

    Imagine opening a box and in it discovering some very old documents. There is a set of detailed drawings of military pennants and insignia, obviously for the battalions of a foreign army. There is a series of notes on the movements of troops. Finally there's an official letter on headed notepaper signed by the Commander in Chief Home Forces, General Sir Harold Franklyn.

2. This experience really happened to a man called Richard Sluman. He was sorting through the belongings of his father a few days after the funeral. Mr Sluman senior had been a quietly spoken country vicar who was greatly respected in the village where he'd served for many years. Yet, judging by the evidence in the box, he'd obviously lived a second, secret life.

    Following some research, Richard discovered that his father, during World War Two, had been part of the British section of the largest resistance movement in western Europe. Even though they never saw active service, this resistance organization consisted of highly trained Special Units, expert in combat and demolition, with a sophisticated network of intelligence gathering Special Duties groups. The members of these groups were largely older, respected people in the community who had reason to travel freely around the countryside. Reverend Sluman was a co-ordinator for such a Special Duties group.

3. A fictional example of someone with a secret life must be Clark Kent. Most of the time he is a mild-mannered, bespectacled reporter, one of the crowd. That's until the word goes out that some catastrophe has happened, someone needs rescuing or the world itself is in danger. Then Clark Kent turns into Superman, the saviour of all things good and wholesome. When the problem has been solved, he reverts to his private persona and no one is any the wiser.

4. I believe that there are also some secret lives being lived out here in this school. For example, there are the quietly successful, those who shy away from publicity and are naturally self-effacing. Their achievements may not be in the obvious arenas of sport and performance, yet are of the highest possible standard. (*You may wish to name an example of such a student.*)

Then there are the quietly generous, the students who give their time and money to support a special cause. Often all they receive is a word of thanks from those they help. Sometimes they may not even get that. (*You may wish to name an example of such a student.*)

Finally there are those students who, without mentioning it to anyone, are secretly living a life of difficulty, maybe even suffering. This could be because of a medical condition that causes them pain or disability. It could be because they are a carer, looking after their parent or siblings in the absence of other support. (*It is probably not appropriate to name an example of such a student.*)

And all this happens in secret.

 Time for reflection

One of the skills that Jesus possessed was that of picking out individuals from among the crowd. He identified the secret concerns of many who came to listen to him and gave them healing and encouragement. He praised the poor woman who secretly gave the last of her money to the temple offering. He identified the traitor among his band of followers. It's a very useful skill.

I'm sure many of you know about one another's secret lives. You also know why these lives are kept secret. So what might be an appropriate way to respond? Even if someone wishes to stay out of the spotlight it's always encouraging to give a personal word of congratulation. A simple thank you to those who are generous can also be appropriate. With those who are suffering or under the stress of caring it may be necessary to be more tactful. A quiet offer of support at the right moment, or a sign of empathy could be all that's needed, but be careful not to cause embarrassment.

Spend a moment considering the following thoughts. You may wish to turn them into a prayer:

Be thankful for those who recognize what you do and give praise, support and thanks.

Be sorry for your own insensitivity to what might be happening in lives around you.

Make a plan to take some action that arises out of today's assembly. It's likely to consist of saying the right words at the right time.

 Suggested music

'He who would valiant be' (*Come and Praise*, 44)

The theme to *The Dam Busters* film (widely available)

'Nimrod' from the *Enigma Variations* by Elgar, a moving piece associated with commemorating those who died in wars. It is played at the Cenotaph on Remembrance Sunday.

SOMETHING FROM NOTHING
We all have something to contribute

By Helen Redfern

Suitable for Key Stage 3

Aim

To show the students that we always have something to offer, however small.

Preparation and materials

- Bible reading: 2 Kings 4.1–7.

Assembly

1. If *X Factor* auditions were held in (*your town*) for your age group, how many of you would apply?

   If *Britain's Got Talent* came to (*your town*), who would go along to the audition?

   If David Beckham wanted to set up a football academy here in (*your town*), which of you would go for a trial?

2. Some of you are really good at singing or have a particular talent or are gifted at football. But most of us are not. Some of you will be sitting there feeling that you are not good at anything. There's nothing you can do. You have nothing to offer.

3. The woman in our story today literally had nothing. The story is from 2 Kings 4.1–7.

   Her husband had died and left her with massive debts. She had nothing to live on, let alone any spare money to pay off his debts. The men demanding the cash were threatening to take her two sons as slaves if she could not pay up. What a desperate situation she was in!

   There were no benefits available or Citizens' Advice to turn to in those days. In desperation, the woman went for help to a man of God called Elisha. Interestingly, he did not just give her what she needed and solve the problem for her. He got her to look at what she had and how she could use it.

'Tell me, what do you have in the house?' he asked her.

It's as if he wanted to help her to help herself. The woman answered, 'Your servant has nothing in the house, except a jar of oil.'

What use could a jar of oil possibly be? She couldn't cook anything with it without ingredients. What on earth could she do with it? Surely she would never get the money and save her boys from slavery with just a jar of oil! But Elisha told her to collect empty jars from all her neighbours and to start pouring oil from her jar into the empty vessels.

Everyone around her would have thought she was mad. It must have taken a lot of courage to go through with the plan. However, she did exactly as Elisha had said, and miraculously she was able to fill all the jars with oil. She could then sell them, pay back the money her husband owed and live off the rest.

She had a little, virtually nothing. But when she started using it, it became something more, and the solution to her problem.

4. Sometimes we can feel just like this woman, with nothing to give. But everyone has some ability, however small. It takes courage to use the little we have, because we are scared of being laughed at. But as we begin to use and develop our small talent, it can grow into something amazing, just like the jar of oil.

 Time for reflection

Let us take some time to reflect on the abilities and positive characteristics that we each have.

(*Pause*)

Let us now think about how we can use all that we have for good.

(*Pause*)

Listen to the words of this prayer and make them your own if you would like to.

> *Prayer*
> God,
> Thank you for the talents that you have given me.
> Help me to see the value in all that I do.
> Help me to use all that I have.

Help me to encourage others to use their gifts positively for good.
Thank you that with your help we can turn nothing into
something.
Amen.

Song
'Make me a channel of your peace' (*Hymns Old and New*, 328)

SUSTAINABLE DEVELOPMENT 1
HOW EVERYONE CAN HELP
Personal responsibility

By Claire Lamont

Suitable for Key Stages 4 and 5

Aim

To look at the idea of sustainable development, and see how we each can contribute.

Preparation and materials

- Prepare three readers (you could use up to 12 if you give each reader one paragraph).
- Download the music 'Fragile' by Sting.
- You might also make up a PowerPoint montage of relevant photos. Try:
  http://images.google.co.uk/images?hl=en&q=pollution&gbv=2

Assembly

Reader 1: Exams are tough. You have to go through a lot of hard work: late nights, stress, no time to see friends or just relax in front of the TV. Why on earth would we put ourselves through that? And yet most of you will work hard, and you will get the results you want through a lot of late nights and stressful days. Why on earth would you do that, when you could be in the park or watching TV?

Reader 2: You do it because you know it will benefit you in the future. You get good results, you get the job you want, or you go to the university you want.

Reader 3: This is what sustainability is about: the future. Living sustainably means making small sacrifices now, for the sake of the people who are going to live on our planet for (hopefully) thousands of years in the future.

Reader 1: As a civilization our current way of life is, in many respects, unsustainable. This is because we cannot continue as we have been doing indefinitely – we cannot sustain it. We are dependent on fossil fuels, which will run out (perhaps not too far in the future); we produce more carbon dioxide than the natural carbon cycle of our planet could ever support, thus leading to climate change; and we produce and distribute food in such a way that the rich in the West get ever fatter, while the poor in undeveloped countries starve to death.

Reader 2: Sustainable development is a way of looking for solutions to these environmental concerns which, at heart, is about the search for equity (fairness) across the generations – ensuring that generations in the future have access to the same resources, and therefore quality of life, as we have now. But it also encompasses the idea of equity within the generations – so it looks for a way of spreading out resource use now more fairly between different countries, whether developed or undeveloped.

In fact, the term 'sustainable development' was first coined by the UN World Commission on Environment and Development in 1987. Its chair, Gro Harlem Brundtland, defined it as development which 'meets the needs of the present without compromising the ability of future generations to meet their needs'. The UN now points to three differing strands to sustainable development: *economic development* (i.e. growth, particularly in those countries whose economies are currently classed as undeveloped); *social development* (i.e. an improving quality of life for all citizens of the earth, whatever their background, race or class); and *environmental protection*, which is probably the idea of sustainability we are most used to.

Reader 3: How can such an ambitious project be realized? *Can* it ever be realized? Obviously, a lot of this issue can only be solved on an international, political scale. But personal choices can have a huge impact. Here are some of the minor things you can adjust in your everyday life that will cut down your carbon use.

Reader 1: Recycling waste instead of throwing it in the bin, and putting leftover food on the compost heap instead of throwing it away.

Reader 2: Using public transport, cycling and walking whenever possible. Cars are huge emitters of greenhouse gases and guzzlers of oil, and we are going to have to shift to seeing them as more of a luxury than an everyday necessity. If you do need to drive, organize car-pooling, where you share a car with your friends or family. Many councils now run their own car-pooling schemes so people can look up others in their area going on a similar journey and get a lift with them, so cutting down the number of cars on the road.

Reader 3: Insulation: encourage your parents to invest in double-glazing, and better wall and loft insulation if they can. This will mean less energy will be lost in heating; it will also save them money on the bills.

Reader 1: Encourage your parents to buy efficient machines: buy hybrid cars if you can, and look for washing machines and dishwashers that are marked with the fuel efficiency sticker. When using the washing machine, turn it down to a 30 degree cycle. And when you're replacing the boiler, switch to a fuel-efficient one (this will save money again!).

Reader 2: Eat less meat, particularly beef. Huge swathes of rainforest are cut down every day to make grazing space for cattle; these cattle then consume vast amounts of food and pass out tonnes of methane (a potent greenhouse gas) before they are slaughtered. Then they are transported thousands of miles to arrive in our supermarkets. The whole process is carbon-intensive and wasteful in a way that producing vegetables is not. You don't have to go vegetarian; just cut down on meat to once a week, and drink less milk.

Reader 3: If you want to go further, there are other things you can do to help: campaign, write to your MP, go on marches and demonstrations. Show governments that this is the most important issue we as a civilization have ever faced, and we will not let it be brushed aside. You could also calculate your own 'carbon footprint' on a carbon calculator (you can do this online), and start to work on bringing that footprint down. Another thing you could look at is 'carbon offsetting' flights and high-carbon activities, if they can't be avoided – this is where you pay to have the carbon you produce 'offset' by planting a tree elsewhere.

Leader: We are all going to have to make adjustments to our lifestyles to cut down on our consumption. They're small sacrifices, like the ones you make before an exam; but the good they will do in the long term for the environment, and our fellow human beings, makes them worthwhile. And they're sacrifices that will save you money and make you feel more healthy – so not all that bad!

Finally, there are some people who will try to tell you that climate change is a myth, that the science is inconclusive. Aside from the fact that there is now a global consensus that climate change is definitely happening, backed up by UN and independent government reports, not to take action now would be foolhardy in the extreme. It would be to gamble on the future of our civilization and our planet, against overwhelming evidence. If we all do our bit to help, the effect will be overwhelming.

Time for reflection

Play the music and show the montage if you are using one.

Ask the students to consider the ways in which they could change their lives and lifestyle to contribute towards sustaining the earth.

> *Prayer*
> Help us all to take responsibility:
> for ourselves;
> for the mess we make;
> for the pollution we cause.
> May we live as people with an eye to the future,
> being more careful with the world's resources,
> that our world may live.
> **Amen.**

SUSTAINABLE DEVELOPMENT 2
THE POLITICS
Global initiatives

By Claire Lamont

Suitable for Key Stages 4 and 5

Aim

To consider the complicated politics of sustainable development.

Preparation and materials

- You might like to download news pictures of the events referred to in the assembly:
www.planestupid.com
and
www.campaigncc.org
- You need to rehearse four readers, if they are being used.
- Suggested music: 'Fragile' by Sting.

Assembly

Reader 1: Climate change is rarely out of the headlines at the moment. Scientific research grows ever more conclusive, and the headlines more frightening: huge glaciers melting, possibly millions of species facing extinction, and the EU, UN and individual governments announcing ambitious – and some far less ambitious – solutions to the problem.

But 2008 saw a crescendo in media coverage of the issue. While representatives from all over the world met in Poznan, Poland, to discuss preparations for the UN climate change negotiations in Copenhagen in 2009 (which aimed to finalize a post-Kyoto plan of action), protesters marched through central London on Saturday 6 December 2008 to demand an end to coal power and to protest at the planned third runway at Heathrow.

Then, on Monday 8 December, a group called Plane Stupid got all of our attention by scrambling over security fencing at Stansted airport and closing down a runway for a couple of hours. As a result, 52 flights were cancelled, thousands of people were hugely inconvenienced, and the headlines for the rest of the week were full of tales of middle-class protesters who were chuffed that they had been arrested and got their cause in the news.

Reader 2: How should we interpret all these different reactions? Should we put faith in the UN and our government, or should we all be climbing on to runways to demand action?

Reader 3: Although in October 2008 Gordon Brown did announce an ambitious target of reducing the UK's carbon dioxide emissions by 80 per cent by 2050, it was only after pressure from MPs that this was adjusted to include emissions from planes and shipping (two of the largest emitters). Many experts state that these targets simply don't match up to the government's current policies – which include building new coal power stations and a possible third runway at Heathrow. If the government continues with these plans, there is simply no way that emissions will be cut by 80 per cent in 40 years.

Reader 4: So it seems that our government, while being one of the better in the world at setting targets, is maybe lacking a bit at putting those targets into effect. And even if individual governments act decisively to stop climate change and make changes for a more sustainable future, this issue is global. If the UK reduces its emissions by 80 per cent but another country (e.g. India, which is rapidly modernizing right now) increases its emissions by 80 per cent, then clearly we have not solved the problem.

Reader 1: Climate change is an issue that can unite the world. It requires concerted commitment to change from every country on the earth. But it is not as simple as just urging every country to reduce their emissions. Sustainable development asks that we create a fair world not only for generations in the future, but for everyone in our generation now.

Currently, the richest nations of the world use up a disproportionate amount of resources and produce a disproportionate amount of pollution. Countries that are currently undeveloped, and lacking adequate food, water and other basic needs for their people, should not have to make the same sacrifices as the rich, developed countries that are causing the vast majority of the emissions now.

If handled properly, climate change legislation can not only help slow climate change, it can also address some of the inequalities between different countries in the world.

Reader 2: The idea is that undeveloped countries should be allowed to become more developed, to reach the basic living standards that we take for granted here in the developed world. Sustainable development therefore requires rich countries to rein in their consumption of resource, and make use of what resources they have more efficiently (and more cleanly). But it also suggests that the way forward is development for poor nations, in line with the environmental necessities of sustainability: clean energy sources like renewables, greater efficiency, recycling of resources and a general cutting down of the amount of resources used.

Reader 3: How can such an ambitious project be realized? (*Can* it ever be realized?) You might have heard of some global initiatives that are currently being tried out for the first time: a prominent example is 'cap and trade schemes', where companies in the EU, for example, can buy permits for the carbon they produce. If they produce more carbon than their permits allow for, they have to buy more permits on an open carbon market; but if they produce less carbon than their permits allow for, they can sell their permits on to other companies who need them.

This is just one example of how ideas for sustainable development are already having an impact. Others include improvements in transport systems following the introduction of the central London congestion charge; the implementation of large-scale renewable energy sources such as wind farms and solar power; and the building of better-insulated houses (the UK government plans to make all new housing zero-carbon by 2012).

Reader 4: To address the issues of equality in different countries, schemes also incorporate ways to encourage western nations to contribute to development projects in poorer countries, and therefore help them grow in an environmentally stable way. The biggest scheme is run by the UN, and is called the Clean Development Mechanism (CDM).

This scheme functions like the EU cap and trade scheme for companies, but on a national level: countries that go over their carbon limits have to pay a fine to other, poorer countries that do not use up their carbon allowance. This money is then used by the poorer nations to pay for clean development schemes, for example, energy generation using renewable sources. The idea is that undeveloped countries aren't punished by climate change: they are able to develop while rich nations pay for the pollution they have caused.

Reader 1: These schemes are imperfect, new, and prone to problems. While they are clever and interesting ways to solve a huge problem, they don't mean that the problem is solved: far from it. More action is needed, and quicker. As citizens, it is our responsibility to learn about the problems, to think about the ways we can help personally, and to show governments that we care.

 Time for reflection

Show the pictures of the protests, and play 'Fragile' by Sting. Leave time for the students to listen and reflect.

You might like to use these words as a prayer:

Climate change, we all contribute.

> We like our holidays.
> We like warm houses.
> We like to drive our cars.
> We like food from all over the world.
> But what could I do to decrease my carbon footprint?
> How can I help the earth to breathe more easily?

Let the music play as the students leave.

TRUTH WILL OUT
Don't be afraid to be yourself

By Helen Redfern

Suitable for Key Stage 3

Aim

To remind the students that however many lies we tell, the truth will become known eventually.

Preparation and materials

- Download the song 'This is Me' sung by Demi Lovato (*Camp Rock* CD), or some alternative reflective music to play during the reflection.

Assembly

1. People all around us tell lies. Some politicians lie about what they will do for the country if elected. Some film stars lie about their relationships. Some footballers lie about unfair tackles. Some business leaders lie about their tax statements.

   And some people seem to get away with it.

2. Over 400 years ago, William Shakespeare wrote in his play *The Merchant of Venice*:

   Truth will come to light;
   murder cannot be hid long;
   a man's son may, but in the end truth will out.

   'Truth will out.' People still use that phrase today. Time and time again, we read in the newspapers and see on TV lies being exposed, people being found out.

3. In *Camp Rock* (the new Disney Channel film first shown in September 2008), Mitchie discovers this truth for herself the hard way. When she first finds out that she is able to attend Camp Rock, a summer camp devoted to music, she is overjoyed. Her mum has been hired to do the catering and as a result Mitchie gets into the camp at a reduced rate, as long as she agrees to help in the kitchen.

Mitchie is overwhelmed by the famous parents and amount of money the other kids seem to have. She is ashamed of her parents and lies to fit in. She claims that her mum is the managing director of Hot Tunes China. And once the lie is told, there is no going back. Even when her mum comes to introduce herself to her friends, she doesn't admit the truth, but dismisses her as someone who has cooked for all the stars.

But truth will out. When her friend Caitlin discovers the truth and describes her as drowning in her lies, Mitchie justifies herself by saying, 'I just wanted to fit in, OK?'

But it's not OK. When the camp diva Tess Tyler finds out, she publicly humiliates Mitchie and exposes her lies for what they are. Mitchie learns the hard way that it's not all about image, but allowing people to see who you really are.

4. Just like Mitchie, we can get so caught up in our lies, so trapped by our deceit. But we don't have to lie about who we are, or what our family is like, or what we have. Our real friends will accept us just as we are. And then, like Mitchie, we can find the freedom to be ourselves by telling the truth.

Time for reflection

Think of the last time you told a lie. Why did you do it?

Were you too scared to tell the truth?

Were you embarrassed about your family?

Were you worried you would upset someone?

Were you trying to avoid the consequences?

Were you afraid to be yourself?

As you listen to the words of Mitchie's song ('This is Me', see Preparation), take time to reflect on the things that you have lied about. Can you think of one situation in which you are going to tell the truth from now on?

Remember, truth will out.

WE'RE ALL IN THIS TOGETHER!
Living in an interconnected world

By Helen Redfern

Suitable for Key Stage 3

Aim

To highlight the interconnectedness of everyone in the world and to show that we can make a difference.

Preparation and materials

- An inflatable globe.
- Six coloured lengths of ribbon, each 1.5 metres long.
- The song 'We're All In This Together' from *High School Musical*.
- Useful websites:
  www.divinechocolate.com
  www.peopletree.co.uk
  www.christianaid.org.uk
  www.independent.co.uk/environment/green-living/london-joins-national-campaign-to-banish-the-curse-of-the-plastic-bag-400242.html
  www.fruit-passion.com
  www.msc.org

Assembly

1. When you see pictures of starving children in refugee camps, child soldiers with guns in their hands instead of toys, or families sorting through rubbish on landfill sites looking for their next meal, I wonder what you think?

   - What can I do about it?

   - Nothing I can do will make any difference.

   - What's it got to do with me?

   The world is getting smaller. Not physically smaller – it is not actually shrinking to *this* size (*hold up the globe*)! But through television reports and newspapers, the internet and cheap flights, we know more, we see more, we are more involved.

Whether we like it or not, what we do does make a difference.

2. Invite 12 children to stand in a circle at the front. As you say each statement, give each end of a piece of ribbon to children on opposite sides of the circle, thus creating a web effect.

3. By buying Fairtrade chocolate, you can help parents in Ghana send their children to school. The Fairtrade farmers' co-operative Kuapa Kokoo doesn't cheat the farmers by using inaccurate weighing scales, as other buying agents often do. The co-operative invests in projects to improve the farmers' living, health and education standards.

    By wearing organic cotton, you can reduce the environmental impact and severe health problems associated with conventional cotton farming. Conventional cotton grown in China has over 20 applications of insecticide each season. These contain potentially carcinogenic substances that are banned in the US and the EU and that are damaging to the young children who harvest the cotton, to the water supply and to the environment.

    By using low-energy light bulbs, you can play your part in slowing down climate change, which is responsible for the devastation of homes and lives in South Africa by severe flooding. Climate change is happening right now and it's the world's poorest people who are paying the price.

    By reusing plastic bags, you can reduce the huge numbers littering our planet. British shops hand out a staggering 13 billion every year. About a million a minute are used worldwide – and then they're thrown away. But they do not biodegrade, so they do not disintegrate with time. They represent a lethal threat to wildlife, in particular in the oceans.

    By drinking Fairtrade orange juice, you can improve the quality of life in Cuba for people like Esperanza. She says: 'It has been great to change from a mud floor to a cement one. Now I can have furniture and it's so easy to clean. Also, the roof is very important, as nothing gets wet when it rains now. I am very grateful to Fairtrade for making this possible.'

    By eating responsibly caught fish, you can help to guarantee that there will always be plenty of fish in the sea. Because our oceans are being seriously overfished, some fish supplies may disappear altogether, unless action is taken. Overfishing is damaging fishing industries and marine environments all around the world.

4. By playing your part, you can make a difference to how the world works. (*Throw the inflatable globe on to the web and let the children balance it on the interwoven ribbons.*)

Time for reflection

It would be a good visual aid to keep the globe balanced on the web during the reflection, but if this would cause too much of a distraction, then the children could sit down at this point and you could hold the globe.

We're all in this together.
Every person, animal, bird, fish, tree, plant …
Each a part of this amazing world in which we all live.
Or, in the words of Gabriella from *High School Musical*:

(*Play/sing the opening verse of 'We're All In This Together' from* High School Musical.)

We're all in this together.

Songs

'God loves you, and I love you' (http://bussongs.com/songs/god_loves _you_and_i_love_you.php)

'He's got the whole wide world in his hand' (*Come and Praise*, 19)

'We're All In This Together' (*High School Musical*)

WHAT'S BEHIND THE LOGOS?
Sports sponsorship's hidden agenda

By Brian Radcliffe

Suitable for Whole School

Aim

To consider the reasons that lie behind the sponsorship of sporting events.

Preparation and materials

- This assembly is especially relevant for the first week of March (after the Carling Cup final).

Assembly

1. The first major football final of the season is the Carling Cup final. (*Give the result of the game, commenting as appropriate.*) The winners are not only awarded a handsome trophy, they also qualify for the next season's UEFA Cup draw. They are the first British team guaranteed a place in Europe. Through the Carling Cup final.

   (*Pause*)

   A sporting event sponsored by Carling.

   (*Pause*)

   What does Carling produce? (*Elicit the response from the students – beer.*)

2. In fact they're not the only alcohol producers involved in sports sponsorship: we have the Guinness premiership and Heineken Cup in rugby, the Stella Artois tennis tournament, the Johnny Walker golf classic, and you can probably think of other examples. The question is: Why do these companies spend such a large amount of money in sponsoring these events?

3. First, they want to get their brand name into the headlines. There are limits placed on alcohol advertising in the UK, particularly on TV, so renaming a sports event to contain the brand name is a

way to get their name on sports and news channels. The Carling Cup must be called the *Carling* Cup.

Second, there is the linked aim of getting their logo seen. If the sporting venue is crowded with placards and posters then the logo will be constantly flashed across TV screens in live coverage and on the highlights.

Third, there is the intention to link the product with an activity that promotes health and fitness, and is encouraged.

4. It doesn't take us too long to realize that while taking part in sport can be extremely beneficial, sitting as a spectator with a glass or two or three of beer in actual fact has a totally different effect. Is this the kind of sponsorship we should be happy about? Many would suggest not.

5. Most of you in this assembly are not the target of this sponsorship by alcohol producers. It's aimed at those slightly older. Yet you *are* targeted through sports events nevertheless. What about these for starters? The championship, the soccer division below the premiership, is sponsored by Coca-Cola. McDonalds have for many years sponsored track and field athletics for young people. They also sponsor the FA community and coaching schemes and aim to be a major sponsor for the 2012 London Olympics. Pizza Hut sponsors men's and women's hockey and we all know that Walkers crisps are behind Leicester City FC.

The products of every one of these companies come equipped with a healthy eating warning. They're unlikely to be part of the dietary regime for the majority of top sporting competitors. Overindulgence can have harmful effects, just as can happen with alcohol.

5. So how do we deal with the issue of sponsorship? We have first to recognize what's going on. Sponsorship takes place in order to persuade ordinary people like you and me to purchase a product. Our response to this might be a chorus of: 'Who do you think you're kidding?' Then I suggest that we detach the sponsor from the sport. We could refuse to use the sponsor's name when referring to the event. We could certainly refuse to buy merchandise that bears the sponsor's logo. We should enjoy the sport itself for its own sake, especially if we are participants. And occasionally, just very occasionally, we might decide to indulge in a Big Mac, a bag of crisps, even a pint if we're old enough,

because we fancy one, not because we have fallen for the sponsors' clever advertising.

Time for reflection

Spend a moment considering the following thoughts. You may wish to turn them into a prayer:

Be thankful for the enjoyment of a good sporting event.

Be sorry for the times when overindulgence has made you less than fully healthy.

Make a plan to take some action that arises out of today's assembly. It might be to become more of a participant than a spectator.

Suggested music

'We Are The Champions' by Queen

WORST-CASE SCENARIO
Urban myths

By Stuart Kerner

Suitable for Key Stages 4 and 5

Aim

To consider how fear can prevent us living full and healthy lives.

Preparation and materials

- You will need to be confident that the 'urban myths' are not too 'near the knuckle' for your chosen audience. If you would like to substitute different stories an excellent place to start is www.snopes.com
- You might like to read the report from the Living Streets Organization about the number of schoolchildren being driven to school. It can be found at:
  www.livingstreets.org.uk/cms/downloads/0-1-final_backseat_children_report.pdf

Assembly

1. Tell your audience that you would like to read two stories reported in the newspapers. Add that the two stories are quite shocking in their own ways and that they both have something in common.

Story 1

A couple from Newcastle were on holiday in Spain. One day, upon returning to their hotel room, they found that their room had been broken into. Although the couple were a little upset that someone had probably been messing with their stuff, it seemed that the intruders had just looked through their possessions, and they were pleased to discover that nothing was actually missing. They continued with their holiday as normal and thought no more about the break-in.

That is, until a few days later, when they got home, and developed the roll of film that was in the camera. In among the happy snaps of each other on the beach and photos of their sightseeing tours was a picture they had not taken. It was quite clearly the image of two strangers in their hotel room; to be more specific, it was the image of two large strange bottoms, and to add to the horror, between the cheeks of said bottoms the couple could clearly see their toothbrushes.

Story 2
Business travellers are being made aware of a criminal gang that is operating in most major cities and was recently very active in New Orleans, USA.

The crime begins when a business traveller goes to a hotel lounge for a drink at the end of the workday. A person in the bar walks up as they sit alone and offers to buy them a drink. The last thing the traveller remembers, until they wake up in a hotel room bathtub, their body submerged to their neck in ice, is sipping that drink. There is a note taped to the wall instructing them not to move and to call an ambulance.

A phone is on a small table next to the bathtub for them to make the call. The traveller calls the emergency services, who have become quite familiar with this crime. The traveller is instructed by the 911 operator to very slowly and carefully reach behind them and feel if there is a tube sticking out of their lower back. The business traveller finds the tube and answers, 'Yes.'

The emergency operator tells them to remain still, and says that paramedics are already on their way. The operator knows that not one but both of the traveller's kidneys have been stolen while they were drugged – harvested, to be sold for illegal transplant surgery.

2. If told carefully, the chances are that your stories will elicit gasps and nervous laughter from your audience. Remind them that these two stories have something in common. You may like to ask for suggestions.

    Eventually, after your audience has tried to suggest possible links between the two shocking stories, tell them that the common link is quite simply that neither is true!

3. These stories are what we call 'urban myths' – shocking stories that pass from person to person and become exaggerated with each retelling. They are a form of folklore, intended to shock and worry the listener, and since the advent of the internet their number has increased enormously.

Every week a new and more shocking story is sent to millions of people via email – totally untrue but nonetheless worrying – about viruses, criminal activity and violent actions perpetrated against unsuspecting victims. Newspapers pick them up and print many untrue stories as facts, which creates further paranoia.

Deep down we probably know that these stories are untrue or at least wildly exaggerated, but the human mind tends to multiply our fears and cause us to imagine all kinds of harm befalling us.

4. Say that a good example of this is the way schoolchildren are increasingly driven to school by parents worried about the dangers of their being abducted or abused by strangers. Statistically these fears are unfounded, but newspaper headlines and urban myths create a 'climate of fear'.

A 2007 survey concluded that 'a perception that the outside world is both a more dangerous place for children and a less protected one is having a profound effect on the way that parents are bringing up their children'.

The actual truth of the matter is that children are now in greater danger from the increased traffic caused by these worried parents!

'Far more people are killed by strangers behind the steering wheel of a motor vehicle than are killed by strangers on foot. Danger should be removed from children rather than children from danger' (Mayer Hillman, John Adams and John Whitelegg *One False Move ... : A Study of Children's Independent Mobility*, Policy Studies Institute, London, 1991).

5. Comment that many of us are missing out on life experiences because of fear and anxiety. Anticipating problems can paralyse us into inactivity, which is a real shame and a waste of the opportunities available to each of us.

Franklin D. Roosevelt, the President who led the USA into World War Two, once said: 'The only thing we have to fear is fear itself – nameless, unreasoning, unjustified terror which paralyzes needed efforts to convert retreat into advance.'

Pope John XXIII said: 'Consult not your fears but your hopes and dreams.'

Perhaps the next time you hear a terrible tale or read a frightening story in the newspaper or receive a worrying story via email, you will take their advice.

Time for reflection

For Christians life should hold no fear. As the writer of Psalm 27 puts it, confidence in God removes fear and allows us to live a life without anxiety:

> The LORD is my light and my salvation; whom shall I fear? The LORD is the stronghold of my life; of whom shall I be afraid?
>
> When evildoers assail me to devour my flesh – my adversaries and foes – they shall stumble and fall.
>
> Though an army encamp against me, my heart shall not fear; though war rise up against me, yet I will be confident.
>
> One thing I asked of the LORD, that will I seek after: to live in the house of the LORD all the days of my life, to behold the beauty of the LORD, and to inquire in his temple.
>
> For he will hide me in his shelter in the day of trouble; he will conceal me under the cover of his tent; he will set me high on a rock.
>
> Now my head is lifted up above my enemies all around me, and I will offer in his tent sacrifices with shouts of joy; I will sing and make melody to the LORD.
>
> Hear, O LORD, when I cry aloud, be gracious to me and answer me!
>
> 'Come,' my heart says, 'seek his face!' Your face, LORD, do I seek. Do not hide your face from me.
>
> Do not turn your servant away in anger, you who have been my help. Do not cast me off, do not forsake me, O God of my salvation!
>
> If my father and mother forsake me, the LORD will take me up.
>
> Teach me your way, O LORD, and lead me on a level path because of my enemies.
>
> Do not give me up to the will of my adversaries, for false witnesses have risen up against me, and they are breathing out violence.
>
> I believe that I shall see the goodness of the LORD in the land of the living.
>
> Wait for the LORD; be strong, and let your heart take courage; wait for the LORD!

Prayer

Dear Lord,

We pray that you will guard and shelter us from fear and anxiety.

Defend us with your protective shield, that we will be fearful of nothing.

Help us, Father, to change our fear and apprehension into trust and assurance.

Keep us dedicated and unyielding in serving you and in doing your will.

And above all give us your peace.

Amen.

 Song

'Think of all the things we lose' (*Come and Praise*, 57)

WORLD FAITHS

HANUKKAH
Judaism (December)

By Stuart Kerner

Suitable for Key Stage 3

Aim

To consider the importance of Hanukkah for the Jews.

Preparation and materials

- For this assembly you will need a single candle and something to light it with.
- Hanukkah (which means 'rededication') has only five letters in the original Hebrew. In English there are at least 17 ways to spell it: Channuka, Channukah, Chanuka, Chanukah, Chanuko, Hannuka, Hannukah, Hanuka, Hanukah, Hanukkah, Kanukkah, Khannuka, Khannukah, Khanuka, Khanukah, Khanukkah, and Xanuka.

Assembly

1. Begin, if possible, with the lights turned off, before lighting a single candle.

    Ask your audience to imagine what it must have been like before the widespread use of electric lighting. Comment that the light bulb completely changed human existence by illuminating the night and making possible a wide range of human activity.

2. The first electric light was made in 1800 by Sir Humphry Davy, an English scientist. He experimented with electricity and invented an electric battery. When he connected wires to his battery and a piece of carbon, the carbon glowed, producing light.

    Much later, in 1860, the English physicist Sir Joseph Wilson Swan set out to make a practical, long-lasting electric light. He found that a carbon paper filament worked well, but burned up quickly. In 1878, he demonstrated his new electric lamps in Newcastle.

The American inventor Thomas Edison experimented with thousands of different filaments to find just the right materials to glow well and be long-lasting.

In 1879, Edison discovered that a carbon filament in an oxygen-free bulb glowed but did not burn up for 40 hours. Edison eventually produced a bulb that could glow for over 1,500 hours.

3. To those who first saw this it must have seemed like a miracle: at last the setting of the sun, especially in the depths of winter, no longer condemned them to the gloom of candlelight.

    Most religions and belief systems have some kind of celebration or holiday based around lights, be they candles, lanterns, fireworks or bonfires. It is no coincidence that most of these festivals seem to take place at the very darkest time of year, near the winter solstice when days are shortest and nights are long.

    These festivals, and the lights that accompany them, are meant to reassure us that eventually the winter will pass and longer and warmer days will return. Eventually, we will experience spring again.

4. The festival of lights celebrated by members of the Jewish faith is called Hanukkah. It is held on the twenty-fifth day of the Jewish calendar month of Kislev and lasts eight days and nights. This usually, but not always, falls in December.

    Although Hanukkah is a relatively minor holiday in the Jewish calendar, its closeness to Christmas has brought greater attention to Hanukkah and its tradition of gift-giving. Amid the ever-growing flood of Christmas advertising, it may seem especially fitting that the Hanukkah story tells of Jewish culture surviving in a non-Jewish world.

5. *The story of Hanukkah*
    Many years ago, in the year 170 BC, there was a Greek ruler in Syria, called Antiochus Epiphanes. His army conquered Israel but Antiochus didn't want to expel the people of Israel from their land. He did, however, order them to reject their God, turn their backs on their religion, customs and beliefs and start worshipping the Greek gods.

    His armies went into the holy temple of Jerusalem, removed the sacred Jewish objects and replaced them with statues of the Greek gods. This was a time of persecution and religious repression for the Jewish people. There were some who did as they were told, but most of the Jews refused to abandon their religion and become Greeks.

One who refused to convert was Mattathias. He had five sons, and Judah was one of them. Judah and his four brothers formed an army and chose as their name the word 'Maccabee', which means 'hammer'.

After three years of fighting, the Maccabees were finally successful. They drove the Syrians out of Israel and reclaimed the holy temple. The Maccabees wanted to clean the temple and remove the despised Greek symbols and statues, and on the twenty-fifth day of the month of Kislev, the job was finished and the temple was rededicated.

When Judah and his people finished the cleaning, they wanted to light the eternal light – which symbolized God's presence. Once lit, the oil lamp should never be extinguished, but only a small pot was found with just enough oil to light the lamp for a single day. The oil lamp was filled and lit.

Then a miracle occurred, as the tiny amount of oil stayed lit not for a mere one day, but for eight days! That became known as the miracle of Hanukkah.

6. The Jewish people began to celebrate Hanukkah to remember the victory over the Syrians and the rededication of the Jerusalem temple. For eight days, Hanukkah candles shine in the window to brighten the night. Family and friends come to help light the candles in the *hanukkiyah* – a special candlestick with eight branches, plus an extra one which holds the candle used to light the others (nine branches in total). On the first night of Hanukkah, the first light is lit; on the next night another light is added, and so on, until by the eighth night all the lights are lit.

Food cooked in oil is eaten, recalling the miracle in the temple: pancakes, called latkes, made of fried potato and doughnuts called *sufganiyot*.

The people also play a gambling game with a special spinning top called a dreidel. This was used at the time of the Maccabees as a diversion when defiantly teaching their children about the Jewish faith.

Presents are exchanged, songs are sung, and the story is told of brave and resolute Judah the Maccabee.

7. Throughout their history the Jews have been the victims of persecution at the hands of various invaders and rulers, most notably in our own time during the Holocaust when six million Jews were murdered by the Nazis.

8. Ultimately, perhaps the most important message of Hanukkah can be found in the name of the holiday itself: Dedication.

   When Jews have dedicated themselves, through faith and action, often in the face of the most extraordinary adversity, to the pursuit of high religious and human ideals, Judaism has remained strong.

   The need to strengthen and remain true to their religion remains an important challenge to Jews across the world at all times and in each generation.

 Time for reflection

After working a dreadful 16-hour day at the nightmarish Bergen-Belsen labour camp, the Jews became the playthings of the Nazi officers responsible for their 'care'.

Supper at Belsen was invariably some old, stale bread, dreadful thin soup and vegetable fat made into a kind of margarine. This margarine was provided in a huge container which was scraped out as required. When the container was empty the guards permitted the inmates to get into it in order to lick out the margarine stuck to the side.

Watching these emaciated figures scrabbling around desperate with hunger presented the camp guards with endless amounts of amusement and hilarity.

Each time this happened a single inmate remained defiant as this grotesque scene unfolded. Motionless, despite his own crippling starvation, this lone prisoner refused to become part of such a humiliating display, and in some small way his fellow prisoners gained strength from his silent defiance.

But one evening, as cruel December winds blew outside and many victims of the Nazis fell prey to hypothermia and exhaustion, a new twist took place that rocked the inmates to their withered skin-covered bones. On this night the unthinkable occurred.

The one prisoner who had remained so utterly defiant and stoical finally lost his coolness, and as soon as the guards indicated their charges could strip the container of its meagre greasy rations, he virtually dived into it before turning his whole body around and around against the sides of the container like a thing possessed.

What an uprorious spectacle! The guards were weeping tears of laughter as they beheld this Jew, formerly so stately and dignified, reduced to the level of an animal. A feeling of profound contentment swept through them as they beheld this man's resolve crack before their very eyes.

After things had calmed down and the officers had left the block, still howling with laughter and patting each other on the back, the inmates could not bring themselves to look at the one man they had until so recently looked to as the keeper of their collective dignity. That was, until he removed his shirt and began ripping it into strips. Naturally their first thought was that having finally been broken the poor man had now lost his mind.

The man looked up, staring intently at his peers before declaring in a low, portentous tone: 'Do you all realize that this is the first night of Hanukkah?' With that he looked down again at his torn clothing and considered it carefully before finding a particular part soaked with fat and tearing it off.

That night the men of one cell block in one concentration camp lit their makeshift *hanukkiyah*, the wicks formed from the shreds of the margarine-soaked shirt.

Through the dedication of one brave man the miracle of Hanukkah happened once more.

> *Prayer*
> The earth is full of your goodness,
> your greatness and understanding,
> your wisdom and harmony.
> How wonderful are the lights that you created.
> You formed them with strength and power
> and they shine very wonderfully on the world,
> magnificent in their splendour.
> They arise in radiance and go down in joy.
> Reverently they fulfil your divine will.
> They are tributes to your name
> as they exalt your sovereign rule in song.
> *Jewish mystical hymn*

YUAN TAN
Chinese New Year (January/February)

By Stuart Kerner

Suitable for Key Stage 3

Aim

To understand the meaning of Yuan Tan and how it is observed.

Preparation and materials

- If you can obtain some Chinese New Year artefacts (e.g. money envelopes, banners) you might like to display these as students enter the assembly.
- You might ask a student to read the story of the 12 animals.

Assembly

1. Start by saying with a suitably mischievous voice that you are pretty sure that some people in this school are pigs; some are dogs; while others are snakes and rats!

   Ask if anyone can suggest what you're talking about. Hopefully (after some choice ideas!) some kind soul will suggest the right answer: that you are talking about the Chinese zodiac and the fact that some people were born in the year of the pig, some in the year of the dog, others in the year of the snake and so on.

2. Years in the Chinese calendar are marked not only by a number but are also assigned to one of 12 animals.

   The story goes that before he died, the Buddha summoned all living creatures together. Only 12 came to wish him goodbye: rat, ox, tiger, rabbit, dragon, serpent, horse, sheep, monkey, rooster, dog and pig – each of which was rewarded for their loyalty by having a year named after them.

   Each animal has a different personality and this is believed to be the main factor in each person's life that gives them their characteristics, success and happiness through their lifetime.

3. It is said that the legendary Emperor Huangdi invented the calendar in 2637 BC, when he introduced the first cycle of the zodiac.

   The Chinese calendar is based on a combination of lunar and solar movements, and each year begins with the first new moon of the lunar cycle. Festivities last until the Lantern Festival (Teng Chieh), which occurs 15 days later at the time of the full moon.

4. Preparations for New Year – also known as Yuan Tan, the Spring Festival – actually begin on the twenty-third day of the previous lunar month, with a ritual known as 'sending off the kitchen god'.

   This is the god who looks after the home. Each year he is summoned back to heaven to report on the family's behaviour. After offering him a sticky cake or honey – intended to sweeten his mood, as well as to make it difficult for him to speak (in case he was thinking of giving them a bad report) – the family set his image alight, in order to send him on his way.

5. The day before Yuan Tan is spent cooking for the feast. No sharp instruments can be used or, the Chinese believe, you might cut out the good luck from the coming year.

   Houses are cleaned, debts are repaid, new clothes are bought and every effort is made to remove all traces of bad luck remaining from the preceding year.

   The entrance to the home is decorated with calligraphic banners, hopeful messages intended to bring forth good luck.

6. A feast called 'surrounding the stove' is held on New Year's Eve, when the spirits of the ancestors join the living round the family banquet table.

   As in all such festivals, food plays an important role throughout Yuan Tan and dinners tend to be especially plentiful.

   To the Chinese, food is life but it is also health and a symbol of other good things such as luck and prosperity.

7. On this night the children wait patiently for New Year. Parents encourage them to stay awake as long as possible in the belief that fighting sleep will add to their parents' life span.

   After midnight on Yuan Tan the family greet each other, saying 'Kung-shi', which means, 'I humbly wish you joy.'

8. At Chinese New Year celebrations people wear red clothes, decorate poems on red paper, and give children *lai-see* –

good-luck money wrapped in little red envelopes. Red symbolizes fire, which according to legend can drive away bad luck.

People are also especially nice to each other on New Year's Day to ensure good luck.

Firecrackers are set off and lion-dancers re-enact the story of Nian, a mythic beast who appeared to terrorize the countryside.

For 15 days there are parades and celebrations, including the lion dance. The seventh day of the New Year is sometimes called 'everybody's birthday' as everyone is considered one year older as of that date.

Chinese New Year ends with the festival of lights, a pageant of lanterns. Some of the lanterns may be works of art, painted with birds, animals, flowers, zodiac signs and scenes from myths and history. Sometimes a paper chariot is made and burnt.

9. Yuan Tan is celebrated as a time of reunion and thanksgiving. It is also a time to settle debts. A long time ago those to whom money was owed were allowed to demand it back. If by Yuan Tan a debtor has not paid off his creditors, both he and his family will be shamed.

10. It is important for all of us to take stock of our lives at regular intervals and think about those people to whom we owe a debt: friends, teachers, parents and loved ones who care for us.

What have we done in the past year? What decisions would we change given the opportunity? Which aspects of our own lives require some 'spring cleaning'?

11. Wish your audience 'Gung hei fat choi', which means 'wishing you prosperity and wealth' and is the traditional greeting that the Chinese use to welcome in the New Year.

 Time for reflection

Confucius (551–479 BC) was a great Chinese teacher and thinker who died convinced that his teachings had been futile. He would be amazed to know he has been revered throughout China for 2,500 years and that to many people in China his wisdom is absolute truth, even now.

Confucius was a respected teacher who attracted thousands of students. Temples honouring Confucius can still be found throughout China today.

Here are some of Confucius' sayings, the wisdom of which is still as relevant to life today as it was two and a half thousand years ago:

'Better to light a candle than to curse the darkness.'

'Judge not the horse by his saddle.'

'A journey of a thousand miles begins with a single step.'

'He who asks is a fool for five minutes, but he who doesn't ask remains a fool for ever.'

'Be not afraid of growing slowly; be only afraid of standing still.'

'Do unto others as you would have them do unto you.'

Prayer
May Heaven guard and keep you in its protection;
make you strong and healthy;
give you much and send nothing but abundance.
May Heaven guard and keep you,
cause you to prosper, and send you nothing that is not good.
May Heaven send down to you so many blessings
that the day is not long enough for them all.
Amen.

An old Chinese blessing

GUNG HEI FAT CHOI!
Chinese New Year (January/February)

By Helen Levesley

Suitable for Key Stage 3

Aim

To learn how Chinese New Year is celebrated.

Preparation and materials

- You will need three readers.

Assembly

1. We are going to try a little Chinese today. Let's all say together, '*Gung hei fat choi*!' Now turn to the person next to you and say it again: '*Gung hei fat choi*!'

   What do you think we are all saying to one another? Take suggestions. Explain that it's the traditional Chinese New Year greeting and means 'wishing you prosperity and wealth'. All around the world on (*insert date*) people from Chinese backgrounds, and in China itself will all be wishing one another 'Gung hei fat choi!'

2. So what is it all about? We have got three readers who are going to tell you a little bit about this very important festival.

   Reader 1: Chinese New Year is also known as the Spring Festival and it is the most important celebration in the Chinese calendar. The Spring Festival celebrates the start of new life and the season of ploughing and sowing. Agriculture is the most important economic sector of China, employing over 300 million people. China ranks first in worldwide farm output, primarily producing rice, wheat and potatoes as well as peanuts, tea, millet, barley, cotton, oilseed, pork and fish. This makes the festival very important for the coming year; it holds the hopes of many people.

   Reader 2: New Year celebrations start on the first day of the lunar month (the new moon) and continue until the moon is at its brightest. This year it begins on (*insert date*) and comes to an end on (*insert date*). The first week is celebrated with visits to friends and family when particular traditions are followed in order to bring the family luck for that year.

Reader 3: Chinese New Year is the oldest Chinese festival and has many customs. For example, before the start of celebrations, Chinese people spring-clean their houses to sweep away bad luck. On New Year's Eve all brooms, dustpans and brushes are put away so that good luck cannot be swept away. This seems a nice way to usher in good fortune for the year to come.

Reader 1: Just as at Christmas, houses are decorated, often with paper scrolls with good-luck words and phrases on such as 'Happiness' and 'Wealth'. It shows the hope for luck for the coming year for you personally, and for your family and friends. Again, as at other festivals, on New Year's Eve families come together to celebrate and to have a meal together. People will stay up until midnight setting off fireworks to frighten away evil spirits. Red symbolizes fire, which will scare away evil spirits that may harm people in the year ahead, and so people may dress from head to foot in new red clothing. On New Year's Day children will wake up to find a red envelope filled with money and sweets under their pillows left by their parents and grandparents. It must be very difficult not to peek!

Reader 2: The second week ends with the lantern festival, on the evening of the last day. The lanterns are often hand-painted with scenes from history or legend. People hang glowing lanterns at the windows of their houses and carry lanterns under the light of the full moon. A dragon dance often takes place with a dragon made of paper, silk and bamboo held aloft by young men who guide it around, collecting money.

Reader 3: In some countries, especially here in the UK, the festivities are shortened, so that the lantern festival takes place on Chinese New Year's Day and you can see parades with the lion-dancing and brightly coloured lanterns. Key areas in the UK that have large Chinese New Year celebrations are Newcastle, Birmingham and especially London, where there will be a large celebration in Trafalgar Square.

3. As you can see, those celebrations and wishes for the New Year are not much different from our own. But I wish I could wake up on (*insert date*) with some money under my pillow!

4. Finally – turn to the person next to you and say: '*Gung hei fat choi!*'

 Time for reflection

Gung hei fat choi to us all.
A year of peace and tranquillity.
A year of growing up with patience and kindness,
growing nearer to our friends, not further apart,
and of peace in our world.
Gung hei fat choi to us all.

RAMADAN
Islam (movable feast)

By Stuart Kerner

Suitable for Key Stage 3

Aim

To consider the significance of Ramadan to Muslims.

Preparation and materials

- This assembly begins with a brief discussion of fad diets; this can be a sensitive subject around teenagers so exercise judgement in using this material.

Assembly

1. Begin by asking your audience how many have tried dieting, maybe after Christmas or ready for their summer holiday. Follow this up by saying you've been looking into diets and have found some very interesting, if rather strange, examples.

   Have you, for instance, tried the 'Apple Cider Vinegar Diet'? According to devotees of this pound-shedding programme, fermenting apples contain pectin, which is thought to give a kick-start to weight loss. So drink a few teaspoons of apple cider vinegar before each meal, and let the fat-burning process begin.

   Don't fancy that? Well, how about the 'Cabbage Soup Diet'? This low-fat, high-fibre diet claims that those who follow it will drop ten pounds in just one week; that is, of course, if they can tolerate seven days of cabbage soup. According to the diet's devotees, you'll shed impurities along with the pounds.

   Still not impressed? Maybe the 'Breatharian Diet' is more your thing. Breatharians think that eating is merely a habit we have developed and that air and sunlight are enough to meet our needs. By training your body to survive on little or no food, you will become fitter, more invigorated and in greater harmony with the universe.

Wiley Brooks, the founder of the Breatharian Institute of America, claimed he had not eaten for 19 years. Unfortunately for fans of this diet Mr Brooks was allegedly seen by reporters enjoying a chicken pie!

2. For many people, encouraged by the media, their body image plays a large part in who they are and diets offer them the possibility of looking like their favourite celebrities. But perhaps it seems that the whole art of dieting involves a large slice of wishful thinking and hoping against hope. Most doctors would say that eating healthily and regular exercise are much better and more effective than binge weight loss and cure-all diets.

3. For those who follow religions it is important to look after your body, as it is given by God, but it is what is on the inside that counts. For Muslims, *Saum*, or fasting, is one of their most important duties. However, many non-Muslims are often surprised to learn that fasting is not undertaken in order to lose weight, but rather is done for spiritual reasons. It is an act of worship.

4. This time of fasting takes place during the ninth month of the Islamic calendar, called Ramadan. Ramadan remembers the time when the Prophet Muhammad (peace be upon him) received the first revelation from the angel Gabriel of the Qur'an – the Muslim holy scriptures. This happened on the twenty-seventh day of Ramadan – known as 'The Night of Power'.

5. The Qur'an says: 'Eat and drink until you can tell a white thread from a black one in the light of the coming dawn. Then resume the fast till nightfall.' During this time Muslims do not drink, or smoke, and even chewing or biting your nails is not allowed!

   Islamic months are based on the movements of the moon and move forward by ten or eleven days each year. The actual fast lasts for 29 or 30 days, depending on when the new moon is first seen.

   This means that Ramadan can take place in the summer or the winter, so some years fasting is expected for only about 8 or 9 hours and other years it can be as many as 18! The fact is that all adult Muslims are expected to go without food from just before dawn until just after sunset.

6. This special fasting teaches Muslims how important it is to show obedience to God, who they call Allah. Fasting should be

accompanied by prayer, charitable giving to the poor, reflection and the complete reading of the Qur'an.

It builds their character and helps Muslims to appreciate how the poor and hungry suffer. Furthermore, it binds them together with other Muslims who share in the same sacrifice and strengthens the feeling of solidarity among the Muslim community.

7. At the end of Ramadan, Muslims throughout the world observe a joyous three-day celebration called Eid ul-Fitr (the Festival of Fast-Breaking). Eid ul-Fitr falls on the first day of Shawwal, the month that follows Ramadan in the Islamic calendar. It is a time to give to others, and celebrate with family and friends.

On the day of Eid, Muslims gather early in the morning to perform the Eid prayer. After the Eid prayer, Muslims usually scatter to visit various family and friends, give gifts (especially to children), and make phone calls to distant relatives to give good wishes for the holiday. These activities traditionally continue for three days. In most Muslim countries, the entire three-day period is an official holiday. The Arabic greeting given at this time is '*Eid Mubarak*!' which can be translated as, 'May you enjoy a blessed festival.'

8. Although the fasting that takes place during Ramadan has a physical effect on Muslims, it is the effect it has on their whole life that is important. The kinds of diets we discussed at the beginning are short-term quick fixes that more often than not don't work. For Muslims, fasting during Ramadan provides exercise for the soul and is a long-term solution to selfishness, egotism and ultimately spiritual death.

 Time for reflection

A Bedouin was walking with his dog in the desert, carrying a leather skin of water on his shoulder, and crying pitifully as he went along. When asked by a passing traveller why he was crying, he replied, 'Because my dog is dying of thirst!'

'Why don't you give him some of your water then?' the traveller said.

'Because I might need it for myself.'

This traditional Muslim story reminds us how absurd it is to keep things for ourselves 'just in case', when others more needy could use them now. For Muslims fasting is a reminder that unselfishness is God's way. If we all could share with one another how much better the world would be!

Prayer
May your blessings be too many to count
and your worries too few to matter.
May your days be filled with sunshine
and your nights with comfort.
May you never go hungry
and be able to share your gifts.
May God bless and protect you and strengthen you.
Amen.

HOLI
Hinduism (February/March)

By Helen Levesley

Suitable for Whole School

Aim

To understand the meaning behind the festival of Holi and its use of bright colours.

Preparation and materials

- You will need the song 'True Colours' by Phil Collins.
- Images of people celebrating Holi. See:
  www.boston.com/bigpicture/2009/03/holi_the_festival_of_colours.html
  www.holifestival.org/holi_image_gallery.html
  or search for images of Holi on the internet.
- You will need three readers, if you are using them. You could also use students to do freeze frames of the different sections of the story.

Assembly

1. Show the images of people celebrating Holi. What do you think these people are doing? Take some answers – you will probably get something like, they are throwing paint at one another!

    Reader 1: These people are putting coloured paint on one another. They will smear it on their faces, and they will throw different powder colours and water at one another too.

    Leader: Who is doing this? (*Take answers.*)

    Reader 2: These people are Hindus.

    Leader: Where is this happening? They could be Hindus in any country, but these Hindus are in India.

2. Why are they doing this? Again take suggestions. You may well get the right answer.

These Hindus are celebrating the festival of Holi. It is the Hindu festival of colours, but it is also a celebration of spring and new life. It is a bright and lively festival where all sense of any differences is laid aside. Those who are of different castes will celebrate together – men and women, old and young, all join in the throwing of coloured paint. White clothes are worn in order for the colour to stand out even more. It looks like a festival of great fun and excitement. It is not often that you get the chance to throw paint at people!

3. There is, as with most Hindu festivals, a story attached that might be acted out or retold. See if you can work out the moral of the story. This is the main Holi legend.

Reader 2: Holika was a female demon, and the sister of Hiranyakashyap, who was the demon king. He thought that he was very powerful and considered himself ruler of the universe. He felt he was higher than all the gods.

Reader 3: Prahalad was the demon king's son. His father despised him because Prahalad was devoted to the god Vishnu. One day the king asked him, 'Who is the greatest, God or me?'

The son replied, 'God is, you are only a king.' The king was enraged and decided to murder his own son.

Reader 1: But the king's attempts at murder failed at every step. Prahalad was pushed off a cliff, and survived; he was flattened by elephants, and survived; he was bitten by snakes, and survived; he was even attacked by armed soldiers, and still lived. He obviously had someone on his side!

Reader 2: In his frustration, the king asked his sister, Holika, to kill the boy. Holika seized Prahalad and sat in the middle of a fire with the boy on her lap – surely this would finish off the boy! Or so the king thought.

Reader 3: Holika had been given a magic power by the gods that made her immune to fire, so she thought this was a pretty good plan. Prahalad would burn to death while she remained cool. But it's never wise to take the gods' gifts for granted and abuse them!

Reader 1: Because Holika was using her gift to do something evil, her power vanished and she was burned to ashes. But Prahalad stayed true to his god, Vishnu, and sat praying in the lap of his demon aunt, untouched by fire. Vishnu protected him, and Prahalad survived even this torment.

Reader 2: Shortly afterwards, Vishnu killed King Hiranyakashyap and Prahalad ruled as a wise king in his father's place.

To celebrate the story, large bonfires are burned during Holi. In many parts of India, an effigy of Holika is burned as a reminder of her bad ways.

4. So what is the moral of the story? The moral of the story is that good always triumphs over evil and those who seek to torment the staunch, faithful servants of the gods will be destroyed. This is quite a powerful message, and one that is highlighted by the importance of colour and fun in the main act of the festival.

It is comforting to know that those who have been bad will be punished and that good is rewarded. We can all think of stories that are similar, but it makes for an important message: that good will out, in all cases! Even if you are trampled by elephants and bitten by snakes!

 Time for reflection

Prayer

Let me see the good rather than the bad,

and use my gifts in order to do good rather than abuse them for other ends.

Let the festival of Holi show me that being good is the way to really gain the rewards that I seek.

ROSH HASHANAH
Jewish New Year (September/October)

By Helen Levesley

Suitable for Key Stages 4 and 5

 Aim

To understand the purpose of the Jewish festival of Rosh Hashanah and to consider the questions asked by Jewish people at this time of year.

 Preparation and materials

- You can use readers if you wish, or lead the assembly yourself.

 Assembly

1. I am sure you all remember where you were for New Year's Eve, or indeed, you might already be planning what you will do for the next New Year's Eve. I am sure for most people it involved staying up late, either at a party or at home in order to see the New Year in at midnight.

   Can you remember what resolutions you made? How many of you have managed to keep them up until now? (*Take a quick straw poll – probably very few.*) Can you recall what you said you would try to do better? Chances are you can't and there is a strong probability that your resolutions only lasted a few weeks, days or possibly months.

2. Today I want to talk to you about the Jewish festival of Rosh Hashanah, which literally means 'Head of the Year'. It falls during the Jewish month of Tishri, which is around September/October in our calendar.

   It is a very important Jewish festival because, although it is a celebration, it is bound up with serious promises and considerations of the year just passed and it provides a unique occasion for personal development and reflection. Some time just to stop and 'be'. Something that today's society gives us very little chance to do.

3. Jews all around the world will spend the time in and around New Year in times of reflection. It is a time for people to shed light on what their priorities really are. It is a time to ask serious questions about your actions throughout the year.

   As I read these questions out, I would like you to take some time to consider them on your own personal level. I will leave a short period of silence between each one.

   - What is the most meaningful thing in my life?
   - Who in my life means the most to me? How often do I let them know this?
   - What are the most significant things I have achieved in the last year?
   - What do I hope to achieve next year and in my life generally?

4. A great deal of time is spent in the synagogue during Rosh Hashanah. Services will focus on God and his kingship, but also people spend time quietly thinking on their actions over the past year, and they will ask forgiveness for their sins.

   Is there anything that you can think of in the past year that you need to ask forgiveness for? Maybe it is an action, a deed, or just an unkind word to someone. Can you still say sorry? Let's take some time to do that now.

5. Although Rosh Hashanah is a time for reflection, it is not all sadness. The New Year is a time of hope, and after visiting the synagogue, families will return home for a meal, and they will dip pieces of apple or bread into honey. This is a symbol of a sweet new year ahead and of hope within it.

   Think about the start of the school year – what hopes do you have for that? Within all the consideration is the hope that Jewish people will try to do better than the year before. I think that this is something that we can all strive for.

 Time for reflection

Think back to those questions asked before and pray this prayer:

Prayer
Let me see what the most meaningful thing in my life is, and be grateful for it.

Let me tell the most important person in my life how much I love
and appreciate them. Remind me to tell them as often as I can.

Help me to see my achievements as significant, and to be pleased
in them, as they are my achievements.

Give me hope for the future, and for life in general, that it may
be sweet and I can look back on it fondly.

 Song

'Lord of all hopefulness' (*Hymns Old and New*, 313)

WESAK
Buddhism (April/May)

By Stuart Kerner

Suitable for Key Stage 3

Aim

To understand what the Buddha taught and how his life is celebrated at Wesak.

Preparation and materials

- You might like to display a statue of the Buddha. Your RE department may also have additional artefacts such as prayer flags, prayer wheels and singing bowls that can be on show as students enter.

Assembly

1. Wesak (sometimes written Vesak) is often known informally as 'Buddha's Birthday', but is in fact the day on which Buddhists celebrate the birth, enlightenment and death of their founder, Siddhartha Gautama – better known as the Buddha.

   This annual festival is observed by Buddhists across the world and especially in many Asian countries, including Thailand, Cambodia, Sri Lanka, Malaysia, Myanmar, Singapore, Vietnam, Nepal, Indonesia, Hong Kong and Taiwan, which have large numbers of practising Buddhists.

   The actual date of Wesak varies according to the different lunar calendars used in different traditions and the date varies from year to year but generally falls in April or May.

2. Buddha is a Sanskrit word that means 'awakened one'. To many people in the West the Buddha is either a fat, bald, jolly man often seen in oriental restaurants, or is the skinny one with a point at the top of his head, sometimes seen lying down or meditating in 'new age' gift shops.

   They are both, in fact, representations of the Buddha, but different Buddhas. The fat, laughing Buddha emerged from

Chinese folklore in the tenth century. He is called Pu-tai in China and Hotei in Japan, and is said to be a future incarnation of the Buddha, Maitreya.

Theravada Buddhism teaches that there is only one Buddha per age, and the Buddha of our age is the historical Buddha, the person born as Prince Siddhartha Gautama in the sixth century BC. This is the Buddha celebrated at Wesak.

3. At Wesak Buddhists are expected to go to their temples before dawn, when the Buddhist flag is raised. Hymns of praise are sung about the Buddha, his teachings, called *The Dharma*, and his disciples, called the Sangha.

Followers may take simple offerings of flowers, candles and incense to place at the feet of the Buddha. These symbolic gifts are to focus the minds of the faithful on the fact that just as the lovely flowers shrivel away after a short time and the candles and incense soon burn out, so our lives are also going to perish and eventually be destroyed.

Those who attend the temple are encouraged to eat only vegetarian food for the day and are told to make a special effort to cease from killing of any kind. In some countries, for example Sri Lanka, all abattoirs and shops selling alcohol are closed during the festival.

Birds, insects and animals are also released in a symbolic act of liberation, bringing to mind those who are imprisoned, held captive or facing torture.

Buddhists take part in the ceremonial bathing of the Buddha. They pour ladles of water scented with flowers over a statue of the baby Siddhartha. This symbolizes purifying one's thoughts and actions.

Many very devout Buddhists will wear a simple white dress and spend the whole day in temples with renewed determination to observe the 'Ten Precepts' – rules laid down by the Buddha that help people achieve enlightenment.

4. Worshippers are required to listen to monks who give talks and recite verses spoken by the Buddha 2,500 years ago, to appeal for peace and happiness in the world. Buddhists are reminded to live in harmony with people of other faiths and to respect the beliefs of other people as the Buddha had taught.

Followers of the Buddha are very aware that his teachings have a great deal to say to us today in our consumer society.

5. We are bombarded daily with advertisements for this and new crazes for that. The latest games consoles, the newest mobile phone and the coolest trainers. The constant longing for new stuff causes us pain and sometimes makes us do unpleasant things to get them: lying, stealing and cheating. Constantly wanting things and being the victim of these desires creates a continuous sense of yearning that is never satisfied.

6. The Buddha's teachings can be summed up by the idea that all life is suffering when we listen to our desires, and until we realize this fact we will continue to suffer. Listen to this story:

Once a man went to tell the Buddha about his troubles. He described his problems with farming – how either droughts or monsoons complicated his work. He told the Buddha about his wife – how even though he loved her, there were certain things about her he wished to change. Similarly with his children – yes, he loved them, but they weren't turning out quite the way he wanted. When he was finished, he asked how the Buddha could help him with his problems.

The Buddha replied, 'I'm sorry but I can't help you.'

'What do you mean?' complained the man. 'Aren't you supposed to be a great teacher?'

The Buddha replied, 'My friend, it's like this. All human beings have eighty-three problems. It's a fact of life. Of course, a few problems will go away now and then, but soon enough others will arise. So we'll always have eighty-three problems.'

The man responded indignantly, 'Then what's the good of all your teaching?'

The Buddha said, 'My teaching can't help with the eighty-three problems, but it can help with the eighty-fourth problem.'

What's that?' asked the man.

'The eighty-fourth problem is that we don't want to have any problems.'

We may not realize it, but we all have a natural belief that if we try long and hard enough, we can make our problems go away.

And beneath that belief lies an even deeper one: that our life should be free from pain.

Although these beliefs might bring us to practise Buddhism, a life free of worries is not what Buddhism is about. The practice of Buddhism is about becoming awake to the truth of who we are. As we practise, our relationship to our problems may, in fact, become less burdened. But as conditioned beings, living in a messy world, we will always have difficulties. We will always have 83 problems.

7. As Buddhists celebrate Wesak and the life of the Buddha, perhaps we should meditate on the fact that a life spent longing is a life of suffering – perhaps we should recognize that and actually start living.

 Time for reflection

In the Buddha you see clearly a man, simple, devout, lonely, battling for light – a vivid human personality, not a myth. He too gave a message to mankind universal in character. Many of our best modern ideas are in closest harmony with it. All the miseries and discontents are due, he taught, to selfishness. Before a man can become serene he must cease to live for his senses or himself. Then he merges into a great being. Buddha in different language called men to self-forgetfulness 500 years before Christ. In some ways he is nearer to us and our needs. He was more lucid upon our individual importance and service than Christ and less ambiguous upon the question of personal immortality.

H. G. Wells

Prayer
May all beings everywhere weighed down with sufferings of body
    and mind quickly be freed from their illnesses.
May those frightened cease to be afraid, and may those bound
    be free.
May the powerless find power and may people begin befriending
    one another.
May those who find themselves in trackless, fearful wildernesses –
    the children, the aged, the unprotected – be guarded by
    spiritual beings, and may they swiftly achieve enlightenment.

*A Buddhist prayer for peace, included in the prayers on the
Day of Prayer for World Peace in 1986 in Assisi, Italy*

PASSOVER
Judaism (usually coincides with Maundy Thursday)

By Helen Levesley

Suitable for Whole School

Aim

To understand the link between Passover and freedom.

Preparation and materials

- Images from the 'Deliver Us' section of the film *The Prince of Egypt* showing elements of the Seder plate (eight). This is during the early part of the film.
- You will also need either two readers and eight people to hold up images, or use PowerPoint to show these images.

Assembly

1. I would like you to close your eyes for a little while. Now just take a second to relax. The best thing about our imaginations is that they can take us anywhere. I want us to go back to a time long ago. I want you to imagine that you are a slave. You work for a cruel master, who makes you struggle on when you feel you can work no more. Even when you finish your day's work, and go home, you don't really feel that you are safe there. Those around you treat you as a second-class citizen, and you have to practise your religion in secret. Friends and family are beaten if they do not respond correctly. You desperately want to get out of this country where you are held prisoner, you want to get to the Promised Land. You desperately want to feel hope, but when you try to think what it might be like when things are better, you don't want to hope too much, just in case it does not come true.

2. Now, open your eyes. How did that make you feel? (*You may like to take responses.*) Trapped, lonely, upset, sad, angry? Maybe all of those things, including many more emotions. I could be talking about any time in our history, black slaves in America,

people imprisoned for their beliefs or even Christians after the time of Jesus. However, I am going to talk to you about the time when the Israelites were slaves in Egypt.

3. Around this time of year (March/April) Jews celebrate one of their key festivals: Passover, or Pesach. It recalls the story of Moses and how he led the Israelites to freedom from the slavery and persecution they experienced in Egypt.

    Moses is a key figure for the Jews and this is why they celebrate the festival of Passover. It recalls when Moses came to Egypt with a task from the Lord. He was to go to the Pharaoh and say to him: 'Let my people go.' Pharaoh was of course proud, and knew that he needed his slaves to build Egypt and make it great. He refused. God sent plagues on Egypt to persuade Pharaoh: of water turning into blood, a plague of locusts, of darkness, of boils, and other things. Still the Pharaoh refused to let the Israelites go.

4. After nine plagues a final one was sent. This was a plague that would surely make the Pharaoh change his mind. The Angel of Death was to pass through the land, and kill all the first-born male children. The Israelites were given special knowledge from God that if they sacrificed a lamb, and painted its blood over the doorframes of their houses, the angel would 'pass over' their homes, and they would be spared. This would show them that they were God's chosen people.

    They did what they were instructed, and the angel passed over their homes, but all the first-born boys of the Egyptians were killed, including the son of the Pharaoh. Having lost his child, Pharaoh finally released the Israelites and told them to leave Egypt.

    The story can be found in the book of Exodus in the Bible. The word 'exodus' itself means evacuation or flight. They were in such a hurry to leave that they did not have time to let the bread they had made for the next day rise, and so they took the unleavened flatbread with them for provisions.

5. The Jewish festival of Passover recalls this very event: the passing over of the angel of death and the liberation of the Jews from their slavery in Egypt. The festival lasts for seven or eight days, and in Israel the full eight days are observed as rest days. In non-Jewish countries, it is only two days, the first and the last.

On the first night of the festival, each Jewish family comes together for a special meal, called the Seder meal. Seder means 'order' and the ceremonies are done in a particular order. Special plates and cutlery are used that are kept exclusively for Passover.

6. The Haggadah is a book that tells in 14 steps the story of the Jewish experience in Egypt and of the Exodus and revelation of God. It contains songs, blessings, psalms and the Four Questions, all of which are read and sung during the meal.

As the story of each of the ten plagues is read out a drop of wine is spilt to remind Jews that their liberation was tinged with sadness at the suffering of the Egyptians.

Children are central to the festivities and there are special games which are meant to hold their attention. In fact, it is the youngest child who asks the Four Questions during the Seder meal. The purpose of the questions is to show the importance of the symbolism:

Reader 1: Why do we eat unleavened bread?

Reader 2: Unleavened bread or matzo is eaten to remember the Exodus when the Israelites fled Egypt with their dough to which they had not yet added yeast.

Reader 1: Why do we eat bitter herbs?

Reader 2: Bitter herbs, usually horseradish, are included in the meal to represent the bitterness of slavery.

Reader 1: Why do we dip our food in liquid?

Reader 2: At the beginning of the meal a piece of potato is dipped in salt water to recall the tears the Jews shed as slaves.

Reader 1: Why do we eat in a reclining position?

Reader 2: In ancient times, people who were free reclined on sofas while they ate. Today cushions are placed on chairs to symbolize freedom and relaxation, in contrast to slavery.

Each of the components of the meal is special, and there is a special Seder plate, which contains all of these symbolic things.

7. The eight images are held up by volunteers or shown on PowerPoint, while saying the words:

- Matzo (unleavened bread), which is eaten symbolically three times during the meal.

- A bone of a lamb to represent the lamb that was sacrificed.

- An egg, also to represent sacrifice, but which also has another symbolism. Eggs become harder when they are cooked. So the egg symbolizes the Jews' determination not to abandon their beliefs under oppression by the Egyptians.

- Greenery (usually lettuce) to represent new life.

- Salt water to represent a slave's tears.

- Four cups of wine to recall the four times God promised freedom to the Israelites. Everyone, including the children, drinks from these cups of wine.

- Charoset (a paste made of apples, nuts, cinnamon and wine) to represent the mortar used by the Israelites to build the palaces of Egypt.

- An extra cup of wine is placed on the table, and the door is left open, for Elijah. Jews believe that the prophet Elijah will reappear to announce the coming of the Messiah and will do so at Pesach.

8. The Haggadah ends: 'Next year in Jerusalem, next year we will be free.'

This festival is incredibly important, because it not only recalls the flight from Egypt, it reminds Jews of the times when they have been persecuted in the past, and always reminds them that God will free them from those chains, because they are the chosen people.

 Time for reflection

Prayer
When I feel that I am trapped, give me space.
When I feel that I am persecuted, give me courage.
When I feel despair, give me hope.
When I need someone to look up to, send me a leader.
When I feel there is no one else to help me, remind me that you are there.
Amen.

GURU NANAK
Sikhism (2 November)

By Stuart Kerner

Suitable for Key Stage 3

Aim

To consider the significance of Guru Nanak for Sikhs.

Preparation and materials

- A flipchart or whiteboard might be useful.
- You might like to show an image of Guru Nanak. If you have any Sikh students they may be prepared to lend you a framed portrait. Alternatively you can find good images online:
  http://en.wikipedia.org/wiki/Guru_Nanak
  www.gnssgera.com/images/gurunanakdevji.jpg
- There are five short stories included in this assembly to illustrate Guru Nanak's inspirational qualities. Some could be omitted, depending on the time available. You could ask students to read these.

Assembly

1. Think of the best teacher you've ever had. What was it about them that made them so special? Ask for suggestions and write them up.

    Ideally, you should get answers including 'kind', 'sensitive', 'wise', 'patient' and 'clever'. If not, add these to your list.

2. Comment that for followers of the Sikh religion special teachers are called 'gurus', and the founder of their faith, Guru Nanak, symbolizes for them everything that makes a great teacher.

    Each November Sikhs around the world celebrate the birthday of Guru Nanak, during a celebration known as a *gurpurb*. *Gurpurbs* are Sikh festivals that remember the lives of the ten gurus who revealed the Sikh faith.

3. Sikhs celebrate Guru Nanak's birthday and the other *gurpurbs* with an *Akhand Path*, a reading of the Sikh holy scriptures, the *Guru Granth Sahib*, continuously from start to finish.

   On the day before the birthday, processions are held. These will include singers, musicians and even teams of people demonstrating gutkha – a martial art practised by some Sikhs. The Sikh places of worship – the gurdwaras – are decorated with flowers, flags and posters showing different features of Sikhism. Sikhs join together to sing, pray and eat together.

4. On the morning of the birthday, festivities begin early, at around 5 a.m., with kirtan (hymns from the *Guru Granth Sahib*) and katha (sermons about Sikhism). These celebrations go on until around two o'clock in the afternoon.

   After this, *Karah Parasad* will be served. This is a sweet-tasting food that has been blessed. The congregation will then share a meal, which may be followed by fireworks. Sometimes the festivities last the rest of the day, with prayers and hymns continuing long into the night.

   Sikhs who are unable to visit the gurdwara during the festival will hold a similar ceremony in their own homes.

5. Guru Nanak was born in 1469, at Talwandi, 40 miles from Lahore. As a tribute to him, this place is now called 'Nankana Sahib'; it is in present-day Pakistan. The Guru was born into a culture where everyone was either a Muslim or a Hindu, and there was little love lost between the two religions. An astrologer had predicted that Nanak was a born disciple of God and would achieve spiritual greatness and be recognized by both Hindus and Muslims alike.

6. Return to the words that make a great teacher and comment that you can tick off all of these where Guru Nanak is concerned.

   To illustrate the Guru's *kindness*:

   Nanak's father worried about his son's future, as he did not seem interested in earning money. He once gave Nanak some money and sent him to Lahore to start a business. On the way he came across some hungry holy men, who were meditating. Nanak spent all the money he had to feed them, returning home with only his generosity to show for his trip!

To illustrate the Guru's *sensitivity*:

One morning Nanak failed to return from his ritual bathing. His clothes were found on the river bank and the townspeople concluded that he had drowned. The river was dragged but no body was discovered. After three days Nanak reappeared but kept silent. It was the next day before he spoke and then he made the mysterious statement: 'There is neither Hindu nor Muslim so whose path shall I follow? I shall follow God's path. God is neither Hindu nor Muslim and the path which I follow is God's.'

To illustrate the Guru's *cleverness*:

Nanak did not believe it important to follow rituals and customs mindlessly as they became habits at best and superstitions at worst. He believed that there was just one God, who was almighty and all-powerful. During the course of his travels, Nanak reached the city of Hardwar. Here he came across Hindu priests who, while standing in the sacred River Ganges, were throwing water towards the sun to soothe the souls of their ancestors.

Nanak bent down and began throwing water in the opposite direction. When asked what he was doing, he replied that he was watering his fields in the Punjab, far, far away. His reply was met with ridicule, but Nanak apparently told the priests that if the water they were sprinkling could reach the sun, then undoubtedly the water could also reach his fields, which were just a few hundred miles away.

To illustrate the Guru's *patience*:

Nanak's travels took him to the Muslim holy city of Mecca. When he arrived in the city, exhausted and hungry, Nanak lay down, and was rudely awoken by a Muslim priest, who asked, how Nanak dare sleep with his feet pointing towards the sacred Ka'aba – the cube structure in Mecca that is the centre of the Muslim world. Nanak responded by asking the priest to turn his own feet wherever God could not be found! The priest had no answer.

Finally, to illustrate the Guru's *wisdom*:

One day Guru Nanak visited a poor carpenter called Bhai Lalo. He enjoyed his host's simple food very much. He stayed for some days.

There was also a very wealthy man called Malik Bhago who lived in the same village. To show off his money he laid on a big banquet. He invited many people to this feast including Guru Nanak. But Nanak refused to go. Malik Bhago came to the Guru and said, 'Why don't you come to my rich feast? Am I no better than a poor carpenter?'

Nanak replied, 'Not at all. I see no differences between any man. I like simple food so I stayed with Bhai Lalo. If you insist I will come to your feast.'

So Guru Nanak went to the feast. He took with him some simple food from Bhai Lalo's house. When the rich food was served, but before anybody started eating, Guru Nanak stood up. He held in one hand the simple food that he had brought from the poor man's house. In the other hand he took the rich food from the feast. All the people looked at him in surprise. He squeezed the two foods. From the poor man's food came drops of milk and from the rich man's food fell drops of blood. All the people were amazed.

Malik Bhago was very angry. He asked Guru Nanak why he had performed this magic. Guru Nanak said, 'This is not magic, this is the truth. A poor man's food is clean. He works hard for it. That is why milk runs out from it. Your food is not clean. You do not get it by honest work. You mistreat the people who work for you. You squeeze their blood. That is why blood has come out of your rich food.'

Malik Bhago could say nothing. He bowed before the Guru and promised to be kind to the workers and to work honestly with his own hands.

7. In 1539 Guru Nanak passed away, and was succeeded in turn by nine more gurus who preached and taught with what they believed to be the direct word of God.

It must be remembered, of course, that although Sikhs respect and celebrate the lives of the gurus as prophets, they do not worship them. In addition, most Sikhs honour prophets and teachers from other faiths, for instance Jesus and the Buddha, as genuine messengers of God.

For Sikhs God is the one true Guru and it was God who taught Nanak when he disappeared under water for three days.

8. In order to avoid the chance of raising any human guru to divine status, the tenth guru ordered that after him there should be no more human gurus, but the holy scriptures would be enough to teach Sikhs the right way to live. That is why the *Guru Granth Sahib* is still given the same respect as the other ten gurus.

9. Truly inspirational teachers like Guru Nanak are rare, but the qualities they instil can be felt through the devotion their followers give to the faith they have inspired.

 Time for reflection

> *There is but One God, His name is Truth, He is the Creator, He fears none, He is without hate, He never dies, He is beyond the cycle of births and death, He is self illuminated, He is realized by the kindness of the True Guru. He was True in the beginning, He was True when the ages commenced and has ever been True, He is also True now.*

> *Guru Nanak*

Prayer
God judges us according to our deeds,
not the clothes we wear:
that Truth is above everything,
but higher still is truthful living.
Know that we achieve God when we love.

Sikh prayer for peace, included in the prayers on the Day of Prayer for World Peace in 1986 in Assisi, Italy

THE BIRTHDAY OF GURU NANAK
Sikhism (2 November)

By Helen Levesley

Suitable for Key Stages 3 and 4, or Whole School

Aim

To discover how Sikhs celebrate the birthday of Guru Nanak.

Preparation and materials

- For a picture of Guru Nanak, see:
  www.en.wikipedia.org/wiki/Guru_Nanak
  www.gnssgera.com/images/gurunanakdevji.jpg
  or ask your RE department.
- You will need two readers.

Assembly

1. Who has a birthday on 2 November? (*Chances are that you will get at least one hand.*) Well, a very happy birthday to you! Did you know that you share your birthday with nearly 18 million people? However, you also share your birthday with someone very special to Sikhs. You share a birthday with their founder, Guru Nanak. However, Sikhs may also celebrate his birthday in April. How good, to be able to have two birthdays!

2. Sikhism is the youngest of the six main world religions, and was founded by Guru Nanak: he was born in 1469, to a middle-class Hindu family in the Punjab region of Pakistan. At this time there was conflict between Hindus and Muslims about whose religion was best. Guru Nanak, after much discussion with various holy men and debating his ideas, discovered a new kind of teaching. This came about after he had disappeared while bathing in a stream. Although the river was dredged, no body was found.

3. After three days, Nanak returned. For one day he was silent, but after that he pronounced that he had been to the court of God and had had direct experience of him. The only path to follow was not either Hindu or Muslim, but the path of God. He had

had a profound religious experience in which his whole outlook and the way he viewed life also changed.

4. Modern-day Sikhs still follow his teachings that there is one God and that every person has a part of God within them.

Listen to the following small sections of his teachings, and think about how you might be able to follow them in your own life:

Reader 1: There is no rich or poor, male or female, no high caste or low caste before God. (A caste is the section of society to which you belong by birth.)

Reader 2: It is through actions that someone comes to God.

Reader 1: As fragrance dwells in a flower, a reflection in a mirror, so does God dwell in every soul. Seek out God, therefore, in thyself.

5. It is right then that Sikhs should celebrate the birthday of their founder. Guru Nanak was the first of ten human gurus in Sikhism and each has a special day. These days are known as *gurpurbs* and they are celebrated with much enthusiasm and excitement by Sikhs. What is involved in this kind of celebration?

6. Sikhs celebrate *gurpurbs* with an *Akhand Path*. This is where a team of readers will read the Sikh holy book, the *Guru Granth Sahib*, from beginning to end without stopping. It takes 48 hours to complete and the readers usually take it in turns and read for two to three hours each, including reading through the night! The reading ends on the day of the festival. Quite a long time, but this is seen as a way to worship and show a Sikh's devotion. This will usually happen at the gurdwara, the Sikh place of worship.

7. The gurdwara plays an important part in the *gurpurbs* too. On the day of Guru Nanak's birthday, it is delightfully decorated with flowers, flags and lights. Sikhs will join as one in the gurdwara and wear their best clothes. They will also join together in the langar, or communal dining area, and have a meal together to celebrate the birthday of their founder.

Time for reflection

I want us to think back to the experience that changed Guru Nanak so profoundly. I am sure you can all think of experiences that you have had that made a difference or changed your outlook on something. Think about that experience now, and think how you acted afterwards. Guru Nanak found that his experience affected him so much that he felt that he needed to lead others to follow his path.

Listen again to two of the many teachings that Guru Nanak gave us:

Reader 1: It is through actions that someone comes to God.

Reader 2: As fragrance dwells in a flower, a reflection in a mirror, so does God dwell in every soul. Seek out God, therefore, in thyself.

Take these ideas out with you into school today, and try to think about what they mean. I hope that the peace Guru Nanak found will come into your life today.

DIVALI
Hinduism (October/November)

By Stuart Kerner

Suitable for Key Stage 3

Aim

To consider the importance of Divali for Hindus.

Preparation and materials

None required

Assembly

1. Divali is a very special occasion for Hindus throughout the world. It is a festival celebrated in India and across the world on Amaavasya, that is, the fifteenth night of the month of Kaartik (October/November).

   The word 'Divali' comes from the Sanskrit word *deepavali*, meaning a 'row of lights'. This festival can be called Divali, Diwali, Dipavali and Deepavali, among other possibilities.

2. Like Christmas for Christians and Hanukkah for Jews, Divali is considered to be a festival of lights, taking place as it does at the darkest time of the year. Traditionally, it is notable for the lighting of *diva* lamps, which are made from clay and filled with oil or liquefied butter.

3. Divali is a time when Hindus take stock of their lives, and look forward to the future. Business people, for instance, check that their books are in order, pay off debts and review their accounts for the coming year. Hindus also clean their homes, wear new clothes and give charity to the needy.

   The many ceremonies associated with Divali are a symbol of the personal journey Hindus are expected to make through their lives, as well as the qualities that should be encouraged for self-enlightenment.

4. The origins of the festival are unclear, being bound up with various Hindu myths and stories. One of the most common

stories about Divali, taken from the holy scripture known as the Ramayana, is the return of Rama and his wife Sita after their 14-year exile. It tells the tale of how Lord Rama, with the aid of the monkey warrior, Hanuman, conquered the evil king Ravana and rescued his wife Sita, who had been captured.

Another story behind the origin of the festival is that Lord Krishna slew the evil king Narakaasura at Divali. Narakaasura used to capture beautiful young women and imprison them. It is said that he kidnapped 16,000 princesses! Eventually, their cries for rescue were heard by Lord Vishnu, who came in the form of Krishna and destroyed the evil king.

Others suggest that King Mahabali is remembered during the festival of Divali. He was a very ambitious ruler who controlled heaven and earth and he never refused any request. Some of the gods pleaded with the god Vishnu to reduce his power, so Vishnu came to earth in the form of Vamana the dwarf.

The dwarf approached King Mahabali and asked if he would give him the space that he could cover with just three strides. King Mahabali agreed, and at this point the dwarf changed into Vishnu and his three strides covered the earth, the sky and the whole universe!

As a result, King Mahabali was sent to the underworld. Lord Vishnu, however, granted him one wish because of his generous character. Consequently, Mahabali is allowed to visit the earth for one day a year, at Divali, and his followers light *divas* and join in joyful celebrations at his return.

5. Whatever the real story, the festival of Divali reminds Hindus to wake up from the sleep of ignorance and to pursue knowledge and wisdom. As light drives out darkness, so should knowledge drive out ignorance.

   Through learning, people are expected to move forwards to the stage of enlightenment in which they realize that God is the Light of lights, and that God brings warmth, love and illumination to all beings and therefore there can be no light greater than God.

6. The aim of Divali celebrations is to get people to start moving along the spiritual path and eventually achieve enlightenment by becoming one with God.

   As they light the lamps in their houses, those celebrating Divali are reminded to light the lamps of wisdom, goodness and an inner awareness of God in themselves. It is through this that they can reach the 'Light of lights' – God.

 Time for reflection

Prayer

May the light of love and devotion shine brightly in your hearts.
May the light of understanding shine in your minds.
May the light of harmony glow in your home.
May the light of service shine forth ceaselessly from your hands.
May the light of peace radiate from your being.
May your presence light the lamps of love and peace wherever you go.

A Divali blessing

Index